The *BEAVER*

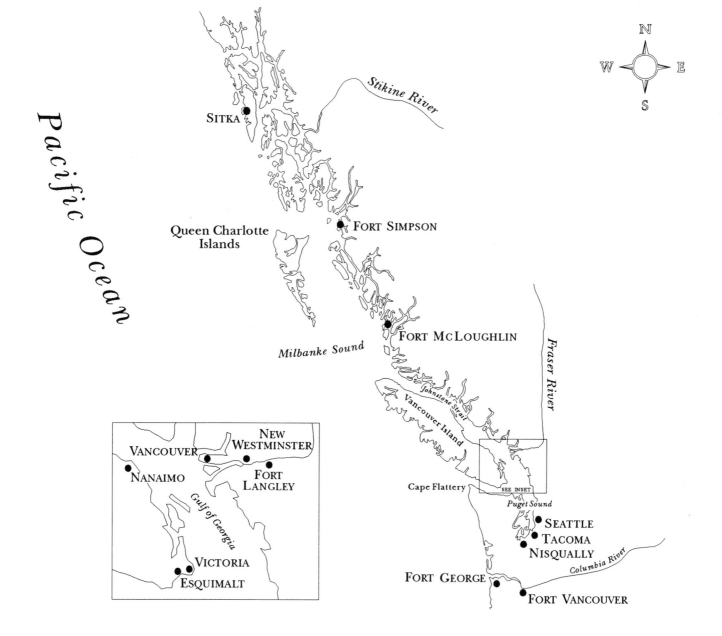

Area of the Pacific coast served by the *Beaver*

First S

Horsdal & Schubart

Horsdal & Schubart Publishers Ltd.
4252, Commerce Circle
Victoria, BC, V8Z 4M2

Front-cover painting "*Beaver* entering Victoria Harbour, 1837",
    by Gordon Miller. Courtesy of Gordon Miller.
Back-cover photograph shows the *Beaver* aground, *ca* 1889, in
    Vancouver Harbour. Courtesy of Vancouver Maritime
    Museum.
Map by Clover Point Cartographics Ltd., Victoria, BC.
Plans of *Beaver* © 1993 by John McKay.
Typeset by Trade Typesetting, Victoria, BC.
Printed and bound in Canada by Kromar Printing,
    Winnipeg, Manitoba.

Canadian Cataloguing in Publication Data

Delgado, James P.
    The Beaver: first steamer on the West Coast

ISBN 0-920663-20-6

1. Beaver (Steamboat). 2. Steamboats—
British Columbia—Pacific Coast—History.
I. Title.
VM395.B43D44 1993   387.2'044   C93-091359-0

Contents

Map
Acknowledgements
Introduction

Chapter One:
THE FUR TRADE   1

    Highlight: The Beaver   4

Chapter Two:
THE FIRST STEAMER ON THE COAST   5

    Highlight: How Much Fuel?   7

Chapter Three:
AFTER THE FUR TRADE   13

    Highlight: *Beaver*'s Captains   16

Chapter Four:
RELICS   25

    Highlight: The Second *Beaver*   32

Chapter Five:
ARCHAEOLOGY OF *BEAVER*   34

Chapter Six:
THE STEAMER *BEAVER*   38

    Highlight: Characteristics of *Beaver*   46

Footnotes   50
Bibliography   52
Index   53

ACKNOWLEDGEMENTS

Several friends and colleagues made this book possible. Leonard McCann, Curator Emeritus of the Vancouver Maritime Museum, created a major travelling exhibition, "The Honourable Company's *Beaver*", in 1977. His companion booklet, of the same title, and Leonard's many files and hours of research were invaluable resources. The staff of the Hudson's Bay Company Archives, housed in Winnipeg at the Provincial Archives of Manitoba, were extremely helpful, particularly Provincial Archivist Judith Beattie. The Governors and Committee of the Hudson's Bay Company granted permission for the various quotations from their archives cited in this book. Mrs. P.M. Coleman, Director, and Ms. Fiona Tait, Archivist, of the Birmingham Public Library in Birmingham, England, provided access to and granted permission for the reproduction of *Beaver*'s machinery drawings in the Boulton and Watt Collection. I am also indebted to the Fort Vancouver Regional Library, and Fort Vancouver National Historic Site, both in Vancouver, Washington, the Washington State Historical Society in Tacoma, and Fort Langley National Historic Site, a Canadian Parks Service unit at Fort Langley, British Columbia.

Access to the Vancouver Maritime Museum's substantial collection of *Beaver* materials was facilitated by Joan Thornley, Caroline Larsen and Shirley Sutherland. Documentation of these artifacts, recovered from the wreck between 1888 and 1973, was undertaken by Derek Kowalchuk under the auspices of the Vancouver Maritime Museum, with photographic documentation by Michael Paris. Funding for the documentation of *Beaver* artifacts, notably the boiler, was provided by the International Brotherhood of Boilermakers, Iron Shipbuilders, Blacksmiths, Forgers and Helpers, Local 359, and the British Columbia Heritage Trust.

Fred Rogers shared details of his 1960-1964 dives on the wreck and dived with Thomas F. Beasley and the author on September 14, 1991, to point out site details, 31 years to the day from his first dive on the wreck. The survey of the wreck of *Beaver* was conducted as part of a larger assessment of Howe Sound and Burrard Inlet by the Underwater Archaeological Society of British Columbia. I particularly want to thank Tom Beasley, Mike Paris, and David Stone of the UASBC.

The graphic reconstruction of *Beaver* was greatly aided by research by Raymond Aker, Leonard McCann, Gordon Miller and John Mckay. I am particularly indebted to John McKay for his outstanding plans of *Beaver*, and to Gordon Miller for his painting of the steamer.

I am also grateful for the editorial eye of several friends and colleagues who read the manuscript in its various editions. Last, but certainly not least, I want to thank Marlyn Horsdal and Michael Schubart of Horsdal & Schubart, publishers of *Dauntless St. Roch*, for keeping the faith and publishing this book as part of a series on the historic vessels of British Columbia.

Any errors and omissions are the sole responsibility of the author.

DEDICATION

This book is for Len McCann, who inspired it, and for Ann Goodhart, who encouraged me to write it.

INTRODUCTION

Between 1836 and 1888, the tiny steamer *Beaver* plied the waters of the Pacific Northwest. For much of its 52-year career, *Beaver* carried the flag of the Hudson's Bay Company, the pre-eminent fur-trading and mercantile operation of North America. Whether trading for furs, escorting scouting parties, or carrying passengers, *Beaver* ranged far along the shores, rivers and inlets of the northwest coast. The steamer's ports of call included Fort Vancouver (now Vancouver, Washington) on the Columbia River, Nisqually on Puget Sound, Fort Langley, New Westminster, Victoria, Nanaimo, Vancouver, Nahwitti, Fort McLoughlin, and Fort Simpson in British Columbia, and Sitka, Alaska.

After brief service as a passenger-carrying vessel, running from Victoria up British Columbia's Fraser River during the gold rush of 1858-1860, *Beaver* was chartered by the Royal Navy. Serving as a hydrographic survey vessel, *Beaver* carried on the important task of charting and mapping the thousand miles of sounds and inlets that form the coast of British Columbia. This task had begun with the voyages of James Cook and George Vancouver in the 18th century. Less than a century later, *Beaver*'s officers completed the work initiated, with lead lines and sextants from the thwarts of cutters and launches, by their predecessors.

At the end of its career, the steamer was employed as a workaday towboat by private operators. Little suggested then that the scarred decks and sturdy paddlewheels of *Beaver* were those of the first steamship to navigate the Pacific coast of North America. However, when wrecked in 1888 at the Lions' Gate, at the entrance to the port of the rising city of Vancouver, *Beaver* became the stuff of legend. The steamer's timbers, fastenings and fittings were wrenched from the hulk to become souvenirs and relics of a vessel that, many felt, was the most significant ship in the history of the west coast.

Many of these pieces ultimately found their way into the collections of the Vancouver Maritime Museum, which now hosts the largest collection of "Beaverabilia" in either Canada or the United States. These pieces range from the massive boiler, both paddlewheel shafts, and a huge sidelever from the engines, to numerous spikes, drifts, and fragments of the hull. They include more than a dozen frames, or ribs, a four-foot-long section of bulwark, cabin doors, furniture fashioned from the ship's timbers, and a few dozen walking sticks. There are other souvenirs made from pieces of *Beaver* — the gavel used to open the first session of British Columbia's parliament in its new buildings in Victoria, and numerous medals cast from copper and brass recovered from the wreck between 1888 and 1891.

Divers rediscovered the wreck of *Beaver* in the 1960s, and their recoveries spurred the study of the steamer by the Underwater Archaeological Society of British Columbia and the Vancouver Maritime Museum. Their goal of protection and study of *Beaver*'s remains, and the return of *Beaver*'s boiler to Vancouver in 1992, serve as reminders that *Beaver* is still a compelling and fascinating subject. It remains so whether people thrill to the saga of the fur trade as visitors to the restored Hudson's Bay Company forts Vancouver and Langley, sail the coastal routes that *Beaver* traced, or learn about the ship through books or exhibits in Oregon, Washington or British Columbia.

James P. Delgado
Vancouver, British Columbia
March 1993

CHAPTER ONE: THE FUR TRADE

For over two centuries, the furs of animals served as the greatest commodities of trade between the New World and the Old. The rich harvests of furs, introduced to European and Asian markets through a complex system of trappers, hunters, traders, and shippers, ensured many fortunes. The fur trade gave rise to commercial empires that spanned the North American continent, probed the Arctic, and sent vessels to the farthest reaches of the rugged west coast of Canada and the United States.

The fur trade began in the early 17th century as the first European settlers, particularly the French, traded for furs with the Indians. Excursions for fur carried Europeans, primarily the French, into the heart of the American continent. The royal colony of Canada was established by France in 1664 with the fur trade as its only business. The Hudson's Bay Company, an English firm, competed with the French, beginning in 1670, and within 20 years was a force to be reckoned with. French competition in the trade lasted until 1760, when France surrendered Canada to Britain with the signing of the treaty that ended the Seven Years' War. Britain then became the major force in the North American fur trade.

While Russian traders had begun to exploit the furs of seals in Alaska during the first decades of the 18th century, it was the actions of British seamen that opened the northwest coast of America to the world fur market. British explorer James Cook's 1778 voyage to the coast induced a maritime rush for fur in the years following his success in selling sea-otter skins bartered for on the coast at a 1,800% profit in China. This seagoing fur trade flourished in the 1780s and 1790s, and lasted well into the 1840s. It brought a number of competing American and British vessels to the coast, and introduced the Hudson's Bay Company to the Pacific.

The Hudson's Bay Company

The potential for profits from the North American fur trade inspired the creation of one of the largest and most powerful business concerns on the continent: the Hudson's Bay Company. Chartered in 1670 by Charles II as the "Company of Adventurers of England trading into Hudson's Bay," it was granted authority to exploit the resources of a tremendous area on the continent, including the shores of Hudson Bay, the Arctic, and vast areas of what eventually would become Canada and the United States. The Hudson's Bay Company, also known as the "Honourable Company," not only controlled a large territory, but also had the power to make and enforce laws, build forts, and maintain military forces to protect its trade. The company's motto, "Pro Pelle Cutem," (Latin for "a skin for a skin") was a play on words that reflected the fact that the company's traders risked their own skins to gather furs. To a few wags, H.B.C. stood for "Here Before Christ."

During the first decades of the 19th century, the Hudson's Bay Company began to seek Pacific outposts, moving west to tap the rich fur-bearing regions defined by the great rivers that drained into the Pacific. The fur trade along the coast was a powerful incentive to expand, but others had already arrived and stood in the way of the company. John Jacob Astor's American firm, the Pacific Fur Company, and the North West Company of Montreal had pioneered the fur trade of the far west. British interests bought out Astor during the War of 1812, leaving the North West Company as the H.B.C.'s greatest obstacle to Pacific trade. A merger of the two companies in 1821, enforced by the British government to halt physically violent confrontations between the two concerns, brought to the H.B.C. all of the North West Company's posts.

Fort George, the former American fort at Astoria at the mouth of the Columbia River, served as interim headquarters for the H.B.C.'s new Department of the Columbia until 1825, when a new post was established farther up river at Fort Vancouver. This fort was the principal Pacific entrepot of the fur trade from the 1820s through the 1840s. Traders and trappers from inland posts came down river, bringing bales of pelts to exchange for supplies and trade goods. From Fort Vancouver, all of the company's furs from the American and Canadian coast were shipped to England. The ships that sailed to England with the furs were sent back each year with trade goods for the coast that Fort Vancouver then distributed on its coasting vessels to outlying trading posts and forts.

To maintain the essential link between England and the Pacific coast by sea, the Hudson's Bay Company employed, either through purchase or charter, 16 vessels in the 30-year heyday of the Department of the Columbia. The first was the six-year-old, Bermuda-built, 161-ton brig *William and Ann*, purchased by the H.B.C. in May 1824 and sent to the coast in July 1824. The company had decided to purchase and send their own ship after "finding the freight asked for vessels on charter to the Columbia rather high...." [1]

William and Ann arrived at the mouth of the Columbia River in April 1825, remaining on the coast for several months before returning to London. The brig was sent north to seek sites for coastal trading outposts, all part of an H.B.C. policy to compete directly with the large numbers of American traders working off various vessels. While the effort was at first hampered by a lack of men and supplies, *William and Ann* made a return voyage to the coast in 1826-1827, and in 1826, workers at Fort Vancouver began the construction of a small sloop, *Vancouver*, for the coastal trade. The sloop remained incomplete for several years, not making a voyage until 1831.

The coastal trading effort, as well as the annual supplying of the Department of the Columbia, was dealt a serious blow when *William and Ann* was wrecked at the mouth of the Columbia River on March 10, 1829, with the loss of the entire crew and the majority of the cargo. George Simpson, in charge of the North American operations of the H.B.C., wrote to the company's offices in London that "the melancholy fate of the *William & Ann* deranges all our plans in regard to the business of the coast for this year...." [2] To offset the loss, the company decided to replace *William and Ann* quickly. The chartered vessels *Cadboro* and *Dryad* were deficient, so the H.B.C. bought the brig *Isabella*.

Isabella was also unfortunately wrecked; the captain mistook his bearings while entering the Columbia River and grounded the brig on a sand bar on May 3, 1830. *Isabella* was a total loss, along with a fair portion of the cargo, as it broke up over the course of the next week. The loss of this second vessel was a serious blow to the fortunes of the H.B.C., but it persevered. The sloop *Vancouver* was sent out on a number of trading voyages, including one to Hawaii, but on March 3, 1834, *Vancouver* was, in the words of the company's official report, "driven ashore on Point Rose, Queen Charlotte's Island, where the natives took possession of the wreck, appropriating the same, with the goods on board, to their own use, and with some difficulty and hesitation permitting the crew to escape, who got to Nass in their boat." [3]

While philosophical about the loss of the sloop, noting in fact that "nor are we in a condition to bring the natives to account for the seizure of the property, indeed we rather feel they behaved well in permitting the crew to escape with their lives," the company needed another ship. [4]

A New Steamer

The problems of sailing vessels on the coast compelled the H.B.C. to examine the relatively new technology of steam propulsion: a steamer was not subject to the whims of tides and winds. The idea of a steamer on the west coast was, for its time, a radical concept. While steamships were operating on the inland waters of Europe and in Britain, in South America, and on the eastern seaboard of the United States, there were none on the Pacific coast of North America.

On August 10, 1832, George Simpson wrote to the company's headquarters in London that "the advantages which a Steam Vessel would possess over sailing craft in navigating the rivers inlets and sounds, which are so numerous on that coast, and where all the trade is made, embolden us...." Simpson allowed that while "the first cost would be heavy," he felt "assured that she would, in a very short time, become the cheapest craft that could be used, and perform more effective service than any two Sailing Vessels...." [5]

Simpson stressed how the steamer could run on its own power up the Columbia River to Fort Vancouver, and up the Fraser River to Fort Langley, the company's two major establishments on the coast. Additionally, "A steam vessel would afford us incalculable advantages over the Americans, as we could look into every Creek and cove while they were confined to a harbour by head winds and calms, we could ascend any stream of any consequence on the coast....in short, a Steam Vessel would, in our opinion, bring the contest to a close very soon, by making us masters of the trade." [6]

Simpson went on to lay out the particulars of the proposed steamer. It should not exceed 180 tons, have a shallow draft to navigate the rivers, and have "machinery of the very best description," although "in order to guard against accident it would be well to have a double set of such parts of the machinery as are most likely to give way...." [7] Simpson was opposed in his request by John McLoughlin, in command of the department at Fort Vancouver, who thought that while "it is true they are the most Convenient vessels we could have on the Coast," steamers were too expensive. [8] If American activity declined, McLoughlin advocated cutting back on the company's outposts and vessels.

John McLoughlin. (COURTESY VANCOUVER MARITIME MUSEUM)

The H.B.C. debated the matter slowly, and in March 1834 notified Simpson that they had approved the construction of a steamer for the Department of the Columbia. The Governors and Committee of the company agreed that the coast was well suited for a steamer, and while expensive, the steamer "will soon be productive of a considerable saving, as she is expected to perform the service of four of the Sailing Vessels now employed on the coast." [9]

Highlight: The Beaver

The beaver (*Castor fiber*), is a large rodent that spends most of its life in the water. There are several subspecies of beaver throughout Eurasia and North America. The North American subspecies are the Canadian, Newfoundland, Rio Grande, Michigan and Golden-bellied beavers. At one time the number of beavers in North America stood at nearly a hundred million.

Beavers live along the banks of lakes, rivers and streams, making their homes in the underbrush. They build dams to slow streams and create ponds or reservoirs, and also construct small houses on banks or in the ponds. A beaver den is a built-up structure of mud and twigs that rises above the water surface. At least two, but at times several, underwater entrances provide the only access to the interior. Some beaver dams are hundreds of metres long and can reach heights of three metres. Always active, these animals inspired the phrase "busy as a beaver."

Beaver pelts were an important commodity of trade. They were so valuable that they were often called "soft gold". Beaver fur is easily made into felt. When stripped from the hide and pressed together with steam or hot water, the fur becomes felted cloth. Beaver felt was the superior medium for the manufacture of hats, and beaver-made hats commanded high prices for three centuries. Beavers also yielded castoreum, two musky-smelling glands near the animal's rectum that were removed and dried for use as a fixative for perfumes or as medicine.

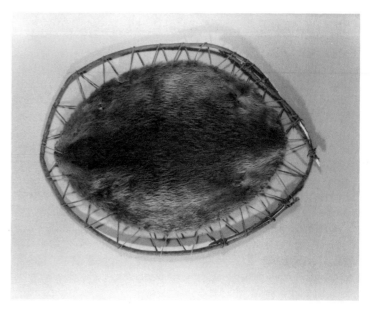

A beaver pelt. (Courtesy Vancouver Maritime Museum)

CHAPTER TWO:
THE FIRST STEAMER ON THE COAST

The contract for the new steamer was let in June 1834 with Messrs. Green, Wigrams & Green, a shipbuilding firm long associated with the Hudson's Bay Company's maritime endeavours. The firm's Blackwall yard had inspected and fitted out vessels chartered and bought by the H.B.C., including *Isabella*, and had already built another vessel for the company. Green, Wigrams & Green also surveyed and repaired many of the H.B.C.'s sailing fleet, and, in addition to the new steamer, were contracted to construct a barque, *Columbia*, for the company. The firm agreed to build the steamer "at and after the rate of 16 pounds sterling per ton for 187 tons" for a total price of £2,992. [1]

The steamer was laid down at Green, Wigrams & Green's yard at Blackwall on the bank of the Thames between the East and West India Docks, in June 1834. By September, work had progressed on the hull. On September 20, it was reported that "Messrs. Green & Wigrams are now raising the frame of the Vessel," so the H.B.C. ordered the machinery for the steamer at a cost of £4,500 from the Birmingham firm of Boulton and Watt, at nearly twice the cost of the hull. [2]

Two 35-horsepower sidelever steam engines, along with a boiler fitted to burn wood and coal, were manufactured for the steamer over a four-month period beginning in late October; 63½ tons of machinery were placed inside the hold before the decks were laid in late February 1835.

Christened *Beaver* by Mrs. John Labouchere, sister-in-law of Henry Labouchere, the vice-president of the London Board of Trade, the steamer, the 218th vessel built by the yard, was launched into the River Thames on May 2, 1835. Fitting out proceeded quickly, and the steam trials were successfully held in the English Channel on June 25. Green, Wigrams & Green launched the 310-ton barque *Columbia* on July 8. Similar in many respects to *Beaver*, but built as a sailer, not a steamer, the barque was intended to serve as the annual supply vessel for the northwest coast. *Beaver* was held ready until *Columbia* was completed and fitted out for the voyage, since the two vessels would sail together.

With her machinery laid up and the paddlewheels unshipped and stowed, *Beaver* departed London's East India Docks for Gravesend. She sailed from Gravesend in the company of *Columbia* on August 29, 1835, for the "Northwest Coast of America," under the command of Captain David Home. The 12-man crew included the mate, W.C. Hamilton, second mate Charles Dodd, chief engineer Peter Arthur, second engineer John Donald, carpenter Henry Barrett, and able seamen William Wilson, George Gordon, William Phillips, James Dick, George Holland, James McIntyre, and William Burns.

The pilot was landed on the 31st, and the two vessels began to beat down the Atlantic. *Beaver*, despite its origins as a steamship, proved the better sailer, and had to slow down to

The Blackwall shipyard, where Beaver *was built.*
(COURTESY VANCOUVER MARITIME MUSEUM)

allow *Columbia* to keep pace. Captain Home, writing to the Hudson's Bay Company, explained that "the *Beaver* is an excellent Sea Boat, & should the Engines go wrong will answer as a sailing vessel perfectly well."[3] On September 30, as the two vessels neared the equator, *Beaver* lost sight of *Columbia*. Arriving off Cape Horn on November 18, *Beaver* hit rough weather, which made the trip around the tip of South America difficult. After a brief stop at Juan Fernandez Island off the coast of Chile, where *Columbia* reappeared, *Beaver* and *Columbia* sailed for Hawaii, arriving on February 4, 1836.

The steamer remained at anchor off Honolulu for three weeks, reprovisioning. This included replacing a thousand gallons of water in the boiler, which had served as a freshwater tank for the voyage. The two vessels sailed from Honolulu on February 25 for the Columbia River. On March 19, *Beaver* and *Columbia* crossed the Columbia River Bar, and anchored off Fort George (Astoria) until the 25th, when Alexander Lattie, an H.B.C. employee who would pilot the vessels up the river to Fort Vancouver, arrived. After a slow passage up the river, *Beaver* arrived at Fort Vancouver on April 10, 1836, 225 days out of Gravesend.

The engines and boilers, partially dismantled by the shipyard for the voyage, were now re-assembled. On May 16, the paddlewheels were installed. That afternoon, at four p.m., the logbook reported that "the engineers got the steam up and tried the engines..." which were "found to work very well."[4] The firing of *Beaver*'s boilers was a significant occasion, because the tiny ship was the first steam-powered vessel to operate on the Pacific coast of North America.

The next morning, the steamer undertook a brief run along the river to collect firewood and to tow *Columbia* to the fort's sawmill. Another brief trip was made on the 23rd. A trip up the Willamette River with "a party of ladies and gentlemen from the fort" followed on May 31, and again on June 5, 11 and 14.[5] Samuel Parker, aboard for the cruise on the 14th remarked that "the novelty of a steamboat on the Columbia awakened a train of prospective reflections upon the probable changes which would take place in these remote regions in a very few years."[6]

First Voyage up the Coast

On June 18, 1836, *Beaver* departed Fort Vancouver under the command of Captain Home, with a crew of 31 persons, including 13 woodcutters. Arriving off Fort George on June 21, *Beaver* crossed the bar on the 25th and headed north for Fort McLoughlin on Milbanke Sound. The steamer never returned to the Columbia River or Fort Vancouver throughout its long career.

On the first trip north, *Beaver* demonstrated one of its least desirable characteristics: a heavy appetite for fuel. George Simpson, travelling on it some time later, noted that *Beaver* carried 40 cords of wood, which was consumed in a day's run. Because it "takes about the same time to cut the wood as to burn it, she is at least as much at anchor as she is underway...." En route to Fort McLoughlin, *Beaver*'s logbook recorded that a few days out of the Columbia, "finding that we had not enough fuel...stopped the steam and made sail to the topsail and unshipped five paddle-blades...."[8] The engines were engaged to bring the steamer into port.

From Fort McLoughlin, *Beaver* steamed farther north to Fort Simpson, before heading through Laredo Channel to Nepean Sound and up to Tongass in Alaska. There the H.B.C. traders met the Russian fur-trading vessel *Chitsekoff*. While the H.B.C.'s intention was to navigate the Inside Passage up to Sitka, as was allowed by an agreement between the company and the Russian-American Company, a Russian officer at Tongass refused permission for *Beaver* to proceed north along the Alaska coast.

Returning south, the steamer stopped at Vancouver Island to check on reports of a deposit of coal suitable for mining. The coal was tested in the ship's boiler and found to

Highlight: How Much Fuel?

Beaver's boilers were built to burn either wood or coal. George Simpson was not exaggerating much when he indicated that *Beaver* spent as much time tied up cutting wood for the boilers as it spent steaming. Chief Factor Duncan Finlayson, writing after *Beaver*'s first trip north, noted that the steamer's supply of 40 cords of wood, which took six "axemen" two days to cut, was burned in a 12-to 14-hour day while steaming some 230 miles. If the various posts and forts did not supply wood, then *Beaver* was delayed for two days "to provide fuel for the consumption of one. In such cases our progress is slow and may be estimated one day with another at 90 miles in three hours or 30 per day." [9] Trader John Dunn, writing in 1844, noted that 26 cords would last *Beaver* three or four days, but his estimate was optimistic.

Coal was expensive and difficult to obtain until the Hudson's Bay Company developed its own coal mine on Vancouver Island in the 1840s. By the late 1840s the steamer rarely, if ever, burned wood and, with the bunkers filled with 20 tons of coal, could steam for days.

At the end of the steamer's working life in the 1880s, second engineer John Fullerton noted that *Beaver* burned ten tons of coal each day, "or rather less than a ton an hour. If she made six or seven knots we considered she was doing well, and five knots was good going with a tow." [10]

be acceptable. From there, *Beaver* headed to Nisqually on Puget Sound, where the crew laid up the steamer for the winter.

Beaver's first trading trip was a successful test of the ship, which was used, in the words of John Dunn, a trader aboard for the ride, "to push on along the numerous and intricate inlets (that interlace the whole country) as far as possible inland, in order to come as much within reach of the interior tribes as possible" for trade. Therefore, "we ran into their uttermost extremities, along almost the whole of the labyrinth" of the coast, "stopping sometimes to trade, and ascertain the capabilities of the country, and the character of the natives, who had never seen a large vessel (and especially a steamer) or a white man before." [11]

On this first trading voyage, the strange new vessel made a powerful impression on the coastal peoples. In 50 years of trade with European vessels, they had never encountered a steamship. One group was so impressed that they built a 30-foot canoe to imitate *Beaver*. It had a black hull with painted ports, a deck, and red paddles turned by an Indian crew who remained under cover. The H.B.C. was satisfied with the steamer; "on the whole she will give the most effectual blow to the [American] opposition...and will also lessen in a great measure the traffic carried on amongst the natives themselves." [12]

Beaver's coastal career commenced in earnest in 1837. Captain Home returned to England, and in his place William Henry McNeill was hired by the H.B.C. as the steamer's master. McNeill, a native of Boston, had arrived on the coast as captain of the brig *Convoy* in 1825, returning in 1831 as master of the fur-trading brig *Llama*. Successful in his trade and in opposition to the H.B.C., McNeill could not be driven off the coast, so the company bought his ship and employed him in its service. A hard-driving man, McNeill took *Beaver* north to the Queen Charlotte Islands in the spring of 1837. Canvassing the coast for furs, he headed south for Nisqually,

William H. McNeill.
(Courtesy Vancouver Maritime Museum)

stopping to examine southern Vancouver Island. In doing so, he discovered the harbour that would eventually serve as the site of Victoria, today's provincial capital.

McNeill actively and aggressively worked *Beaver* on the coast for nearly a decade, travelling thousands of miles, trading for furs and showing the H.B.C.'s flag. The captain's aggressive style brought him into conflict with his men, however, and in 1838 the steamer's crew mutinied.

The mutiny aboard *Beaver* came in late January, in response to the incredible amount of work required to feed the boiler and the crew's dissatisfaction with McNeill, who resorted to blows and floggings to enforce his commands. While off Fort McLoughlin, McNeill sent a note aboard to his engineer, "requesting," in the good captain's words, that the stokers come ashore to help carry firewood down to the beach. The stokers and the seamen, inspired by the engineer of the steamer, refused, despite orders from both Captain McNeill and John Work, the chief trader in charge of the fort. McNeill's problems were compounded when his crew sent a written protest ashore claiming that as an American citizen, he could not legally command a British vessel. The crew demanded McNeill's replacement.

McNeill and Chief Trader Work argued unsuccessfully with the crew for the next two days. As McNeill noted in his report to his superiors, "We thought to put the whole gang in Irons, but as it was absolutely necessary for the vessel to get to Fort Nisqually" and their actions might lead to bloodshed, McNeill and Work decided to have the chief trader replace McNeill as master for the trip south. [13] The crew agreed, and *Beaver* proceeded to Nisqually with Captain McNeill as a passenger aboard his own ship. Arriving in mid-March, *Beaver* was once again left idle because Work announced his intention to return the steamer to McNeill's command and the mutineers once again refused to go to their posts.

The chief engineer argued that McNeill had interfered with the stokers and engineers and had made unreasonable demands upon them. The engineer wanted an agreement that McNeill would leave the engines to the engineers and concern himself with navigating the steamer. McNeill was outraged, noting that he had employed the stokers in extra duties only four times, twice to haul water for their own use, and another two times to haul wood. This he thought reasonable, since the stokers had an extra grog ration and never stood watch, "which the seamen and wood cutters are obliged to do to protect the vessel from attack by the numerous Indians we are always surrounded with...." [14] Work and McNeill were able to force several of the crew back to duty, but they fired a small group they were unable to persuade.

Trading on the Coast

Beaver served as a floating trading post, carrying various goods such as knives, blankets, axes, tobacco, combs, mirrors,

Typical trade goods. (COURTESY VANCOUVER MARITIME MUSEUM)

beads, flints, molasses, and tobacco to exchange for a variety of furs. The steamer's "skin book" records transactions for black, brown and grizzly bear skins, beaver pelts, castoreum, deer and sheep hides, wolf pelts, and the skins of lynx, otters, marten, marmots, mink, muskrats, raccoons, seals, wolverines, and rabbits.

George Simpson described trading aboard *Beaver* in 1841: "The standard of prices being fixed after two hours of haggling, the business then went on briskly. To avoid the inconvenience and danger of a crowd, half a dozen only...were to be admitted on deck at once; and, in order to enforce the regulations, five sentinels were stationed on the gangways, on the poop, and on the paddle-boxes, while the boarding netting...formed a better protection than all the watchmen put together. Stationing himself at the steerage hatchway, Captain McNeill threw down each skin, as he examined it, with its price chalked on it--the equivalents being handed up from below by the two or three men that were in charge of the store." [15]

The fur trade, on an isolated coast and with at times hostile customers, was dangerous business. *Beaver* was armed, to defend the vessel and enforce the company's rule on the coast. Dr. John Sebastian Helmcken, a passenger aboard the steamer in 1850, said "she had the appearance of a small man-of-war, had four brass cannon, muskets and cutlasses in racks around the mainmast, and hand grenades in safe places. Along her sides were boarding nettings...." [16]

Beaver continued in the coastal fur trade through the 1850s. The steamer's skin book shows transactions through 1856, but after 1853, *Beaver* was primarily used as a towboat due to the arrival of the H.B.C.'s new steamer *Otter*. A new era had dawned for the pioneer steamship of the Pacific coast.

In the Company's Service

In addition to trading, *Beaver* also carried company officials on various voyages to explore the coast and for other purposes. After the 1839 season, the boiler was leaking and in bad repair. It was patched sufficiently for a trip north in 1840 with James Douglas, who went to Sitka to negotiate with the Russian-American Company. On this voyage, *Beaver* changed course to run up the Fraser River to the company's outpost at Fort Langley. Fire had raged through the fort, destroying it in April. *Beaver* remained at anchor off the site as workers laboured to build a new fort before sailing on May 5.

Sir James Douglas. (Courtesy Vancouver Maritime Museum)

Douglas' negotiations with the Russians were successful, and in June, his party aboard *Beaver* took possession of the Russians' Fort Stikine before establishing their own outpost at the mouth of the Taku River.

In late August 1841, *Beaver* headed north from Nisqually up the Inside Passage with Sir George Simpson as a passenger. The head of the H.B.C.'s North American operations was in the midst of a tour of the company's empire. Simpson was greatly pleased with *Beaver*, and, in an angry exchange with Chief Factor John McLoughlin, supported using the steamer on the coast instead of building forts and other outposts. Simpson explained that "the mysterious steamer, against which neither calms nor contrary winds were any security, possessed, in our estimation, this advantage over stationary forts, that, besides being convenient for the purposes of trade, she was the terror, whether present or absent, of every tribe on the coast." [17] Simpson decided to close forts McLoughlin, Stikine and Taku in favour of *Beaver*; Chief Factor McLoughlin argued unsuccessfully that the steamer regularly cost, but did not make, money.

Problems with the machinery, particularly the boiler, laid up *Beaver* at Nisqually for much of 1842. Captain McNeill, disgusted with the boiler's problems and *Beaver*'s lack of cargo space, had written to Simpson at the end of 1840 urging that he should either dispose of the steamer or convert it into a sailing vessel. He also recommended that the company build a new, 600-ton steamer to replace *Beaver*. His recommendations were ignored. A new boiler shipped from England in 1842 was installed in the summer of that year, and in March 1843, *Beaver* was sent to Vancouver Island to establish a new post in the harbour discovered by Captain McNeill several years previously at the island's southern end. This depot, created on Simpson's orders, was named Fort Victoria.

The Oregon Treaty of 1846 established the boundary between the United States and Great Britain's Canadian territories. Fort Vancouver, the headquarters of the Columbia department, lay well within American territory, and in June 1849, the company abandoned its post on the Columbia River and relocated its headquarters to Fort Victoria, *Beaver*'s new home port. Boiler troubles laid up the steamer that year, but a new one was installed in mid-October and *Beaver* returned to service. Usually operating in British Columbia waters at this time, the steamer made a trip to Nisqually in 1851 which led to its seizure by American authorities for allegedly landing passengers before formally clearing U.S. Customs.

Painting entitled "S.S. Beaver, *10 miles from Fort Simpson".* (COURTESY VANCOUVER MARITIME MUSEUM)

Presented, 1941, by Ernest Robson, son of Rev. Ebenezer Robson.

Ht. B. Co. Steamer "Beaver"

Hudson's Bay Co S.S. "Beaver". Photo by "C. Gintile, phographer, Victoria".   City Archives. J.S.m 1941

Earliest known photograph of Beaver, ca *1863.* (COURTESY VANCOUVER MARITIME MUSEUM)

CHAPTER THREE: AFTER THE FUR TRADE

The Hudson's Bay Company's gamble on the new steam technology paid off in *Beaver*. With a ready supply of fuel, albeit a slow and tedious task of constantly cutting wood, and with deposits of coal available in British Columbia, the company had a reliable vessel. Capable of reaching any inlet, and not dependent on the vagaries of wind or current, *Beaver* was an ideal floating fur-trading post. With its guns and armed crew, the steamer was also capable of enforcing the H.B.C.'s rule on the coast. It had occasionally done so. In 1852, *Beaver* was used to bring to justice two natives accused of murdering an H.B.C. shepherd on Vancouver Island. In a show of arms, the two men were brought aboard and tried by a jury. They were then executed.

By the 1850s, *Beaver* was getting tired. It was also too slow and too small, compared with steamers then being built. In the late 1840s, the company slowly withdrew its various sailing vessels on the coast in favour of a smaller fleet, primarily composed of *Beaver*, the barque *Columbia*, *Cadboro*, *Cowlitz*, and the brigantine *Mary Dare*, all of which were retired in the 1850s. In 1852, the company decided to replace *Beaver* with a new steamer, which was ordered from Green, Wigrams & Green. The 287-ton propeller steamer *Otter* arrived on the coast in 1853. *Otter* assumed the primary role in the fleet, and *Beaver* was relegated to transporting general freight and passengers on Puget Sound.

Passenger Service

A new boiler was installed in *Beaver* during the winter of 1856-1857. Rumours of gold on the Fraser River during the same year, and a discovery of gold at Hill's Bar in March 1858, led to a rush. By the end of the year, at least 18,000 people had departed from California for British Columbia. Gold seekers sailed up the coast to Victoria, where they then sought passage across the Gulf of Georgia and up the Fraser River to Fort Langley, now an important jumping-off point for the goldfields. *Beaver* was diverted to that service, running from Victoria up the Fraser, until 1860. The usual trip took between 12 and 15 hours to complete.

One gold-rush passenger, Charles Woodard, described his trip aboard *Beaver*: "We stood huddled together for mutual warmth on the afterdeck like cattle.... A small awning covered but half the deck passengers, and afforded but little protection against a driving storm of sleet and snow which followed us from start to finish." Woodard was pleased that the trip was short, and that "the little steamer possessed the merit of staunchness, and she certainly proved as industrious as her patronymic, for she kept steadily buffeting head winds and a very heavy sea until she landed us, drenched, cold and hungry, but withal thankful, at Fort Langley." [1]

One passenger who fared better on the steamer was James Douglas, formerly of the Hudson's Bay Company, who in the summer of 1858 was named the first governor of the new crown colony of British Columbia. Douglas, crossing from Victoria in *Otter*, transferred vessels and ascended the Fraser River in *Beaver* to Fort Langley, where the ceremonies inaugurating the colony were held on November 19, 1858.

Beaver's passenger accommodations were improved in early 1860 when the ship was pulled out for work on the hull; a larger superstructure with cabins was erected on the decks, and the engines were overhauled as well. *Beaver*, noted the editors of the Victoria *Daily Colonist* in their March 27 edition, "looks well in her new dress." The work on the engines and boilers stood the steamer in good stead a few days later, when *Beaver* won a race between Victoria and New Westminster with the steamer *Julia Barclay*.

The steamer's victory was short-lived, however. In May, the owners of the steamers running "in opposition," or as competitors, agreed to pay the Hudson's Bay Company $1,000 a month to keep *Beaver* out of service. Anchored in

Victoria's harbour, the vessel was relegated to duty as a powder hulk, storing gunpowder in her holds, for the next two years. There was no need to use *Beaver*, since the H.B.C. had recently sent a new and larger steamer, *Labouchere*, to the coast. The 680-ton *Labouchere*, built in 1858, arrived in Victoria at the end of January 1859. There, Captain John Swanson, *Beaver*'s master for the past few years, took command of the new steamer. ☙

Royal Navy Service

Beaver's idleness ended in December 1862 when the steamer was chartered by the Royal Navy at a cost of £1,000 per year for use as a survey vessel. Captain George Henry Richards, R.N., in command of HMS *Hecate*, was just completing his tour of duty on the Pacific, where he had actively charted and mapped the British Columbia coast in both HMS *Hecate* and HMS *Plumper*. Richards was following up on the work of George Vancouver, who had first charted the region in 1792. Recalled to Britain to serve as Hydrographer of the Royal Navy, Richards was eager to continue the coastal survey, and he detailed Lieutenant Daniel Pender to command *Beaver*.

The H.B.C. was concerned that the steamer might be placed in dangerous circumstances as a surveying vessel, apparently forgetting *Beaver*'s aggressive forays into every nook and cranny along the same coastline in the 1830s and 1840s. On December 16, 1862, Captain Richards wrote to the company's local representative to assure him that *Beaver*'s risks were few when compared with ocean-going steamers on an exposed coast. *Beaver* "will be merely employed during the summer months, between April and October, in the sheltered waters between Vancouver Island, and the Continent, or in the still more safe, and sheltered navigation of Fitz Hugh, and Milbank [*sic*] Sound...." With an officer in command who had five years' experience on the coast, and with three

Lieutenant Daniel Pender, R.N. (COURTESY VANCOUVER MARITIME MUSEUM)

times as many crew aboard than the company had employed when *Beaver* was in the H.B.C.'s service, "I have therefore no hesitation in affirming that the *Beaver* will be subject to far fewer risks, than even a ship of war would be." [2]

Assurances notwithstanding, the contract between the H.B.C. and the Royal Navy, signed on December 20, stipulated that "in the event of the Vessel being lost wrecked or damaged during the Continuance of this Agreement, the company shall not be bound either to repair her or replace her by another vessel." The concern was not so much with losing the old and tired *Beaver*, but rather being contractually forced to provide the navy with the newer, larger *Otter* or *Labouchere*. The Victoria agent also shrewdly told his superiors in London that Richards' letter "may enable their Honours to insure her at a lower rate than at present in consequence of the risks of navigation being so much diminished." [3]

Beaver was towed from Victoria to the nearby naval depot at Esquimalt to be altered for its naval career. On April 11, 1863, the Victoria *Daily Colonist* explained that *Beaver*, then on naval trials, carried a crew of four officers, 29 seamen, and a marine. The cabins built in the superstructure for passengers now accommodated the officers, a chart room, and a wardroom, while workers built separate cabins for the ship's surgeon and the engineer into the paddlewheel boxes. As befitted its naval status, *Beaver* was armed, but, according to the newspaper, "the only piece of ordnance (if worthy to be considered as such) borne by the vessel is a 1 lb. swivel gun forward."

Beaver commenced its naval career in June 1863. Between then and 1870, the steamer charted and surveyed a thousand-mile stretch of the British Columbia coast, pushing up to Alaska. *Beaver* charted the Fraser River's mouth, and a variety of inlets and sounds both on Vancouver Island and up the Inside Passage. On one survey, Portland Inlet was found to extend 11 miles farther than previously shown on the charts. The steamer's naval crew left the names of its officers on the landscape as new areas were charted. Pender, Bonwick and Blunden islands were named for the officers, as was Coghlan Rock. The ship itself lent its name to Beaver Creek, Cove, Harbour, Ledge and Passage. Historian Derek Pethick also noted that Connis Islet in Beaver Passage was named for the steamer's mascot, a Skye terrier. [4]

The H.B.C. renewed the contract with the Royal Navy each year without change. However, in January 1865, the company's agent, W.F. Tolmie, wrote to London that "We have renewed for one year the lease of the steamer *Beaver* to Mr. Pender acting for Her Majesty's Government, acting on the same terms, and for the same surveying purposes as heretofore. Mr. Pender is of opinion that the *Beaver*'s boiler will require renewal in two years hence." [4] The boiler, always a weak spot in the steamer, was replaced again in 1866 at the H.B.C.'s expense.

The Royal Navy decommissioned *Beaver* on December 20, 1870, at James Bay, off Victoria, and the H.B.C. laid up the ship in 1871, the same year British Columbia joined the new Canadian confederation. In June 1873, the company's Victoria representative recommended selling *Beaver* because the steamer was "old and her upper works considerably weather beaten.... Since she was surrendered to us by the Naval Authorities she has remained at anchor in the Harbour and looked upon as our only resource in case of any accident to the *Otter*...." The possibility of refitting *Beaver* for passenger service had been discarded because "since the imposition of the requirements of the Canadian Steamboat laws, the alterations necessary to qualify her...would cause considerable expense...." The agent asked for authority to sell *Beaver* "as I think some of the saw mill Companies here might make a bid for her, and convert her into a Tug, which she is best adapted for." [5]

Highlight: *Beaver*'s Captains

David Home, 1835-1837
William Henry McNeill, 1837-1844
Charles Humphreys, 1844-1845
Charles Dodd, 1845-1851
Charles Stuart, 1851-1852
William Henry McNeill, 1852
Charles Dodd, 1852-1856
John Swanson, 1856-1858
Herbert G. Lewis, 1859-1860
Lieutenant Daniel Pender, R.N., 1863-1870
George Rudlin, 1874-1875
Thomas Pamphlet, 1876
J.D. Warren, 1877
George Marchant, 1878-1879
John F. Jagers, 1880-1883

Charles Dodd. (COURTESY VANCOUVER MARITIME MUSEUM)

John Swanson. (COURTESY VANCOUVER MARITIME MUSEUM)

Hebert G. Lewis. (COURTESY VANCOUVER MARITIME MUSEUM)

Thomas Pamphlet. (Courtesy Vancouver Maritime Museum)

Beaver Becomes a Towboat

While various parties were interested in the steamer, *Beaver* was finally sold in August 1874 for $15,700 to seven businessmen — John Stafford, George Rudlin, Henry Saunders, Charles Morton, Edwin Coltman, William Harrison, all of Victoria, and Frederick Williams of Esquimalt. The H.B.C. considered it a good sale, since the ship was valued at only $6,000, and their engineer estimated that the new owners would need to spend an additional $5,000 to return *Beaver* to service.

The steamer was re-registered on October 13, 1874, and a week later, the Victoria *Colonist* reported that *Beaver* had steamed for Nanaimo the day before to tow the barque *Whistler*. It was the beginning of the final stage of the pioneer steamer's career. In 1875, the various owners incorporated themselves as the British Columbia Towing and Transportation Company, and *Beaver* was employed at $250 to $350 per tow.

In October 1877, *Beaver* was hauled out by the new owners at the Albion Iron Works in Victoria for much-needed work on the machinery. John Fullerton, the second engineer, explained "she was given a new boiler...not much was done to the engines themselves" except installing new, more efficient steam valves. The superstructure was changed "considerably during the overhaul, and was cut down near the stern" to create a clear space for towing. "Some of the cabins were removed, but she still had many good staterooms down below. I didn't like it there, however, and had one up on deck, just beside the paddlewheel. I well remember the thud-thud-thud of the paddles as they went round beside me." [6]

On October 27, 1877, as *Beaver* returned to Victoria's inner harbour after a trial trip to Esquimalt from the Albion Iron Works' wharf, the Victoria *Colonist* approvingly wrote that the steamer "skimming with the grace of a sea-bird over

Beaver *as a supply boat, stopping at a logging camp,* ca *1887.* (Courtesy Vancouver Maritime Museum)

George Rudlin. (COURTESY VANCOUVER MARITIME MUSEUM)

the surface of the harbour and making the water boil and surge in her wake in great, foam-laden swirls" had made the run in an hour and eight minutes. *Beaver*, the paper concluded, "has performed more hard work than any vessel now afloat and now converted into a tow boat is as sound as a dollar and in better condition than ever for active service."

Beaver's good condition did not last for long. Just three days later, while towing the coal-carrying ship *Henry Buck* up the Gulf of Georgia to load coal at Nanaimo, *Beaver* and her charge ran into strong tides at Dodd Narrows. "*Beaver*'s head swung round and the *Henry Buck* bumped into her," second engineer Fullerton explained. "Her smoke stack fell off, and she was pretty well disabled, as the outer bearing of her paddle-wheel cracked and dropped down." Another steamer took *Buck* in tow, and then returned to tow *Beaver* back to Victoria for repairs. Within a few days *Beaver* was back in service, and towed "our old enemy the *Henry Buck*," as Fullerton termed the ship, from Nanaimo to the strait, "where we cast her off in a fair wind." [7]

Working as a towboat, *Beaver* carried a ten-man crew, with master, mate, two engineers, two firemen, two coal passers, steward, and a deckhand. The steamer towed coal ships to and from Nanaimo, but also towed lumber ships in and out of Burrard Inlet, where the city of Vancouver would soon rise above the forest. *Beaver* also towed log booms, and carried freight, including cattle. According to Fullerton, "If things were slack she would go out to Albert Head and anchor there, and wait for sailing ships to come up from Cape Flattery. The crew went ashore if there was nothing in sight, and I have known her to lie there a whole week waiting. At other times she was very busy." [8]

Beaver's tows also included rafts of logs; one account notes that in the summer of 1881 the steamer was towing logs from various logging camps to a sawmill near New Westminster on the Fraser River. Eugene Thurlow of Seattle, reminiscing in 1953, recalled how he piloted *Beaver* to the mouth of the

Beaver *on the ways at Cook's yard, Victoria, 1877.* (Courtesy Vancouver Maritime Museum)

Nicomekl River to load logs as a young man. The tow took all day, with *Beaver* working at only three knots. The ageing engines, although linked to a new boiler, were not up to the task at times. One former crew member, J.W. Whitworth, claimed that the steam pressure was so low that "we had to stop the engines to blow the whistle." [9]

In February 1883, *Beaver* struck a rock near the entrance to Burrard Inlet and sank. According to the Nanaimo *Free Press* of February 14, at high tide the steamer was "nearly all submerged. The forward part, engine house and the pilothouse is under water, the stern being a little out of the water." The newspaper report was optimistic that *Beaver* would be refloated as it was "a strong staunch vessel, and although well up in years...will stand a good deal of hard buffeting." *Beaver* was raised, but was not refitted for service. That year, in the words of the steamer's last master, George Marchant, who was then serving as *Beaver*'s mate, "business

became very dull, and the *Beaver* was laid up at Victoria, where she partially filled with water and was beached for some time." [10]

The British Columbia Towing and Transportation Company sold the laid-up steamer to one of the company's then-partners, R.P. Rithet, who in turn sold it to Henry Saunders. Saunders sold *Beaver* to Edgar Crow Baker of Victoria in early 1886. In 1887, at Marchant's suggestion, the steamer was pulled off the beach and resumed service for a few months, carrying passengers and supplies between logging camps in 1888 while under Marchant's command.

The Wreck

Beaver went ashore at Prospect Point, near the First Narrows of Burrard Inlet, on the night of July 25, 1888, after departing Vancouver to pick up a load of logs at Thurlow Island. W.H. Evans, assistant engineer, later recalled that "the tide was pretty near high water, but still running in, because the captain hugged the shore pretty tight to get past the eddy off Observation Point, and the first thing I knew she hit, and that settled it. We all got off. We were in a hurry to pack up.... We got off into the water and waded ashore...." [11]

Rumours that captain and crew were intoxicated were never confirmed, despite the fact that the entire group had just left the bar at the Sunnyside Hotel before sailing, and after the wreck hiked back to the hotel to have another drink. Rather, strong inshore currents sweeping along the point, as well as Captain Marchant's close-in course, were the principal causes of the wreck. Salvage was not economical, and *Beaver* was left to disintegrate on the rocks.

Beaver *anchored in Victoria's harbour, ca 1871.*
(COURTESY VANCOUVER MARITIME MUSEUM)

George Marchant. (Courtesy Vancouver Maritime Museum)

Beaver *aground on Prospect Point, Vancouver, ca 1888-1889.* (Courtesy Vancouver Maritime Museum)

CHAPTER FOUR: RELICS

The wreck of *Beaver*, although permanently wedged into the rocks, remained the property of Edgar Crow Baker. The previous owner, Henry Saunders, remained on the scene as manager for the ship. On Saunders' orders, Captain Marchant removed *Beaver*'s bell and binnacle. Unfortunately for Saunders, recovery of pieces of the historic vessel by visitors began almost immediately in 1888. Saunders' daughter later remarked that while "people had no right to go down and tear her to pieces," when her father complained to the police, "they said she was too far out of town that they could not watch her at that distance." [1]

Visiting the wreck of *Beaver* for a Sunday picnic became one of the city's favourite pastimes. Painters set up their easels, photographers took pictures from every possible angle, and the curious climbed aboard to remove pieces from the ship. It was a different process from the usual maritime salvage effort. The history of the vessel was well known, and the removal of items, including innocuous artifacts like Captain Marchant's clay pipe, was inspired by a quest for souvenirs, if not relics of *Beaver*.

Through the years the hulk remained lodged on the rocks, fittings, equipment and timber were stripped from *Beaver*. A.E. Goodman, quoted in the Vancouver *Daily Province* on July 28, 1929, stated that "I have often clambered on her slippery deck at low tide in search of enough teakwood from her sturdy sides to make walking sticks to give to my friends in the east, and each time I ventured on board there were others there with axe and saw on the same errand as I was."

The engines were broken up and in part salvaged for scrap. John Williams, one such salvor, stated that he had blown up the engines with dynamite, and sold the iron to a junk man. However, photographs of the wreck between 1888 and 1892 do not show the destruction that blasting would have caused. The majority of the engine machinery was

Painting of Beaver *aground, "Original sketch from small boat anchored in the Narrows".* (COURTESY VANCOUVER MARITIME MUSEUM)

removed at the instigation of, and by, one man, Charles McCain, a history-minded book seller whose attention was directed to the machinery after the wreck had disintegrated, exposing the hold.

Charles McCain and *Beaver*

Working during extreme low tides in December 1892 with two friends, Edward Brown and James N. Menzies, McCain took away almost everything worth carrying, including the "walking-beams" or oscillating levers. The walking beams in question were the four sidelevers from *Beaver*'s twin engines. Only one of these sidelevers has survived. Found buried beneath the floor of a garage and presented to the Vancouver City Archives in July 1940 by

Beaver *aground,* ca *1890.*
(Courtesy Vancouver Maritime Museum)

Menzies' widow, the sidelever was mounted atop Prospect Point, on the cliff above the wreck site, in July 1941 by the Vancouver Parks Board. It remained there, on outdoor display, until February 1992, when it was transferred to the Vancouver Maritime Museum.

McCain also salvaged bronze and copper fittings and fastenings, which were apparently melted down to manufacture souvenir medallions commemorating *Beaver.* According to McCain, he stripped 1,058 pounds of metal. It consisted of "a vast assortment of copper bolts...several sets of main shaft bearings...various other sets of various dimensions, a variety of copper tubing, several brass plungers, a number of valves and numerous small devices belonging to the ship's machinery, besides two large bronze condenser valves...." [2]

At the end of 1892, McCain reported the wreck's visible remains "at very low tide" were "a section of the bottom, on which rested a few chunks of iron and a promiscuous pile of furnace bricks." [3] McCain identified one of the "chunks of iron" as the intermediate shaft, the centre portion of the

paddlewheel shaft array, a 7½-foot-long casting with 18-inch cranks at either end. Brown drowned, and McCain nearly lost his life while trying to salvage the shaft on New Year's Eve, 1893. McCain managed to retrieve the casting at a later date, and it, too, was melted down.

When McCain's salvage ended in 1893, he devoted his efforts to the production of medals and a souvenir book. Little attention was then paid to the vessel's remains until 1903. On July 9 of that year, the Victoria *Colonist* noted a move "to petition the provincial government to raise the venerable timbers of the steamer *Beaver,* patch them up and place them on exhibition. When the *Beaver* was stranded on the rocks before she fell to pieces, the City Council at Vancouver was urged time and again to have the ship carried bodily to some safe place on land." C.H. Cates of North Vancouver, who

Engine room of Beaver, ca *1889.*
(Courtesy Vancouver Maritime Museum)

Empress of Japan *passing the hulk of* Beaver, ca *1892.* (Courtesy Vancouver Maritime Museum)

Charles McCain's book and medals. (COURTESY VANCOUVER MARITIME MUSEUM)

Medals made by Charles McCain.
(COURTESY VANCOUVER MARITIME MUSEUM)

Beaver spike, and mug made of copper salvaged from the wreck.
(COURTESY VANCOUVER MARITIME MUSEUM)

owned a tugboat yard and a fleet of vessels, offered to do the job for $600 and place the wreck ashore in Stanley Park, but the offer was not taken up.

Attempts to Raise the Wreck

The *Colonist* went on to say that "an attempt was even made by a Victoria man to raise capital to have the boat shipped to the World's Fair [of 1894]. Portions of this steamer...can still be seen above the water at low tide." Other pieces of *Beaver* were placed ashore in the park, among them a lifeboat alleged to be from the wreck, and a section of a mast that was erected in 1913 as a flagpole.

These efforts came to naught, but another salvor recovered additional parts of the steamer's machinery a few years later. C.C. Pilkey of Vancouver, working with an "exclusive privilege," as a partner of Charles McCain's, recovered *Beaver*'s boiler on October 1, 1906, lifting it with a wrecking scow and depositing the 22-foot-long artifact on the beach at North Vancouver.

The boiler was sold by Pilkey in 1909 for $2,000 to the Washington State Historical Society in Tacoma. In October 1908, the *Colonist* had reported that Pilkey was working to recover machinery because "both Seattle and Tacoma are anxious to secure it [*Beaver*] for the purpose of adding it" to the state's exhibit at the 1909 Alaska-Yukon-Pacific Fair in Seattle. "Tacoma," stated the reporter, "is willing to take all the relics and prepare them in an elaborate manner, with electrical and other displays, if given that privilege." [4]

Although sold to the historical society in February 1909, the boiler did not arrive in Tacoma until 1912, after being shipped south on the tug *Annie* and then hauled overland to be placed on display. The boiler remained in Washington until early 1992, when it was purchased by the Vancouver Maritime Museum. With the assistance of the International Brotherhood of Boilermakers, Local 359, the British

Columbia Heritage Trust, Seaspan, and Vancouver Shipyards, the museum barged the boiler back to Vancouver, restored it, and placed it on display in April.

Two large pieces of the machinery that were ultimately recovered as well were the paddlewheel shafts. In 1908, Pilkey's efforts were reported to be directed at "the remaining crank shaft." The other had been "recovered by parties and

Beaver's boiler on display at Tacoma, Washington.
(COURTESY VANCOUVER MARITIME MUSEUM)

The boiler being raised in 1908.
(COURTESY VANCOUVER MARITIME MUSEUM)

melted down." [5] Pilkey salvaged the port shaft in December, stuck in the rocks near the shoreline and visible at low tide, and sold it in 1909, along with the boiler, to the Washington State Historical Society.

A newspaper report in January 1909 from the local steamboat inspector urged the recovery and display of the "cylinders, entablature, and jet condenser" of *Beaver* since "they are almost the only parts that would be actually of the original structure as from the works of Boulton and Watt," and presumably because he believed them to remain at the wreck site. [6] No salvage effort followed, although in August 1925, divers working on the wreck of the tugboat *Radius*, lost near Prospect Point, recovered an old anchor from 80 feet of water. The Vancouver *Daily Province* described it as "a picture of dissolution...deeply cut by rust," with "great sea worms" embedded "in the crevices of rust-eaten metal...." [7] The anchor was identified by the elderly George Marchant, *Beaver*'s last captain, as one of those carried at the steamer's bow.

Divers Rediscover the Wreck

The recovery of *Beaver*'s anchor in 1925 marked the last occasion anyone disturbed the vessel's submerged hulk until 1960, when Fred Rogers, Ed Seaton, Cliff Donovan and

Fred Rogers and Ed Seaton raising a crosshead from Beaver, *1962.* (COURTESY VANCOUVER MARITIME MUSEUM)

Gordon Squarebriggs became the first modern divers to relocate the wreck. Their effort followed a 1951 report from F.W. Pamphlet, the son of one of *Beaver*'s captains, that a "slab" of the wreck remained at the site that presumably could be raised "with grappling irons." [8] Anchoring off Prospect Point on September 12, the four men dived without finding the wreck. When they surfaced, their boat had begun to drift because the anchor line had snapped. Rogers and Donovan went back down to find the missing anchor. Instead, Rogers found wreckage from *Beaver* wedged into the rocks.

Rogers surfaced loaded down with pieces he had plucked from the wreck, telling Donovan "It's part of the *Beaver*... and there are a lot more down there." [9] In those early days of diving on the coast, no thought was given to leaving the artifacts from the steamer on the bottom, or to an archaeological study. The practice of underwater archaeology was new, and the few expeditions undertaken to that time had worked on ancient ships in the Mediterranean. To Rogers and his friends, their discovery was a trove of material from the famous steamer, and they endeavoured to raise as much as they could for presentation to the Maritime Museum.

Rogers returned to *Beaver*'s wreck several times, explaining that he salvaged "brass rods and copper objects" scattered among and embedded in timbers, a bronze rudder fork, pieces of iron machinery, brass valves, and sections of copper steam pipe. Rogers reported that "Many other large pieces of iron remained buried under rocks and gravel..." including "large pieces of an engine...." [10] One piece of iron machinery recovered by Rogers in 1960 was a rod, from its size probably a connecting rod for the air pump, with a connecting strap at one end. In 1962, at the time the starboard paddlewheel shaft was recovered, Rogers also located, raised, and then lowered back to the bottom the crosshead from one of the steamer's engine cylinders.

The Aquaholics dive club, with artifacts recovered in 1972.
(COURTESY VANCOUVER MARITIME MUSEUM)

In April 1964, Rogers returned to the wreck and recovered more brass and copper fittings, as well as an anchor found at a depth of 40 feet. It proved to be his last visit to the site for nearly 30 years. The next diving expedition of record was the Aquaholics Diving Club of Vancouver in February 1972. Relocating the wreck, five divers — Lou Lehman, Maurice O'Neill, Pete Dressler, Uwe Maibauer, and Walter Rudek — swam over a pile of bricks from the boiler, which the divers thought must have been dumped on the site. On two separate weekends the men removed a boat davit, bricks, timbers, more rudder forks, and copper fastenings from the wreck, and reported that they had found "a large section of wood, protected...by a foot of sand and mud" that Lehman wanted to dig out. [11] Those plans never came to fruition, though, and once again the wreck of *Beaver* was left quiet and undisturbed in the depths off Prospect Point.

Highlight: The Second *Beaver*

In 1966, the federal government joined the provincial government and the community to observe the centennial of the merging of the British colonies of Vancouver Island and the mainland to form British Columbia. As part of the celebrations, the Royal Canadian Navy constructed a replica of *Beaver*. Around the metal hull of YSP-126, a 1957-built ammunition lighter, the 137-foot-long wooden hull was constructed at the HMC Dockyard at Esquimalt.

The new *Beaver* was built to approximate the appearance of the original ship. False paddlewheels masked the fact that the ship was driven by propellers. Instead of steam, the new *Beaver* was powered by twin Caterpillar 327 Diesel engines.

After operating on the coast in 1966 and 1967, *Beaver* was retired to Esquimalt in 1968. Berthed at the naval base as a floating exhibit, *Beaver* was refurbished in 1971 and sent on another cruise to mark the centennial of British Columbia's entry into Canada.

Beaver was sold by the federal government in 1972. Passing into private hands, *Beaver* began a new career as a dinner-cruise and excursion vessel operating out of Vancouver. S.S. *Beaver* Cruising Charters is a popular attraction, accommodating as many as a hundred persons for sightseeing, dinner and dancing cruises, and special events such as weddings and meetings.

Last known photograph of Beaver, *showing towboat configuration, with a load of cattle, March 1888.* (Courtesy Vancouver Maritime Museum)

CHAPTER FIVE: ARCHAEOLOGY OF *BEAVER*

The wreck of *Beaver* remained undisturbed, lying submerged off Prospect Point, until 1986, when divers from the Underwater Archaeological Society of British Columbia and the Vancouver Maritime Museum began to survey the remains. Their efforts led to marking the wreck site with a commemorative plaque in 1988; in 1991, they returned to *Beaver* as part of a provincially funded underwater archaeological survey of Howe Sound and Burrard Inlet. Under permit from and for the Archaeology Branch of the British Columbia government, the divers were intending to recover information, not artifacts.

Underwater archaeology is concerned not only with removing pieces of shipwrecks from the seabed; it also works to learn about the past by not disturbing shipwrecks. With measuring tapes, cameras, and sheets of mylar that act like paper underwater, the divers from the Underwater Archaeological Society, working with a professional archaeologist, began to make a map of *Beaver*'s remains.

Since Rogers' 1964 dives, the wreck site has been partially covered by rock added to the shoreline to construct a pedestrian walkway around Stanley Park. Artifacts and portions of the steamer's hull lie buried beneath and between the large granite boulders and rocks. The bottom in this area, at an average depth of 25 feet, is still largely the same rock and gravel on which *Beaver* was wrecked and where its remains were deposited.

The bottom slopes sharply away from the shoreline, dropping rapidly into the 120-foot depths of the main shipping channel. Within a few yards of the seawall, the gravel bottom is at 20 feet; from there it quickly drops at 40 feet to hard-packed sand that continues, with a sharp decline, to the middle of the 200-yard-wide channel.

Down below, in the dark water, divers need to work fast because of the strong currents that sweep through the Lions'

A diver visits the wreck. (COURTESY UNDERWATER ARCHAEOLOGICAL SOCIETY OF BC)

Gate. Diving only at slack tides, when the currents are slow, the divers have at best little more than an hour before the racing waters make it impossible to hang on. Beginning in September 1991, and working sporadically every few months through 1993, the divers searched the bottom for pieces from *Beaver*. Each piece located was tagged, and in time a long rope, or a baseline, was stretched along the bottom to link together every major piece of wreckage.

Every artifact discovered on the bottom was then plotted on a map by measuring its location and distance from the baseline. It is a slow, tedious process, hampered by the fact that in the dark water divers often cannot see each other, and rely on short, sharp tugs on the line to communicate. Every piece of wreckage, from large iron castings to scattered timbers and brass spikes, was plotted. A thick mass of rust mixed with sand and gravel, called "concretion", coats the iron artifacts on the bottom. Concretion distorts the original shape of the iron, and also makes it difficult for divers to tell what is iron and what is rock. Careful observation and repeated dives are the only way to tell the difference.

With every artifact mapped on paper, the spread of wreckage from *Beaver* becomes obvious. Instead of a scattered jumble of wreckage, patterns show how the steamer broke apart, and how its broken hulk settled on the bottom. This is important information, because it tells the archaeologists not only how the currents and tides broke up *Beaver*, but also where to look for other parts of the ship. In mapping the wreck of *Beaver*, the divers also discovered that despite four years of souvenir hunting, blasting, and the strong currents that swept through the wrecked steamer, much has survived. Most of the bottom of the hull remains pinned to the seabed by the remains of the engines and a large pile of bricks from the boiler. Some artifacts show where the starboard side of the hull collapsed and settled on the seabed, while others indicate where the stern tore free and bounced along the bottom. All of this information was gained without picking up or removing a single artifact.

Portions of the wreck. (Courtesy Underwater Archaeological Society of BC)

The Wreck of *Beaver*

The remains of *Beaver* include at least two large sections of the hull. One is a section of oak outer-hull planks, held together by sheets of copper sheathing, that runs out from beneath a cluster of rocks that have obviously settled atop the hull. The remains of an engine keelson lie on the floors, pinned in place by a mass of concretion.

Lying partially on top of the timbers are the remains of bedplates for at least one of the engines, as well as the flattened remains of a hot well, which was a casing fitted on top of an air pump that drew in hot water condensed from steam by the engine's condenser. This hot water was then recycled into the boiler to be reheated into steam. Nearby, a flanged section of seven-inch-diameter copper steam pipe rests next to a large concretion, confirming that this area is an undisturbed section of the engine room aft, or behind the cylinder.

Resting at the approximate 20-foot contour of the seabed, this section of hull is matched by other timbers, some copper fastenings, and two pieces of iron plate in the rocks. The remains of the diagonal stays from the entablature that supported the paddlewheel shafts lie offshore from this section. Flat bands or straps of iron rest at the same level, and are probably remains of the diagonal iron strapping that supported *Beaver*'s hull. The orientation of this section of the hull matches the position of *Beaver* shown in photographs of the stranded steamer, suggesting that despite the strong currents, this portion of the ship's bottom--the engine-room area--is exactly where it came to rest in 1888.

A large pile of bricks lies atop the concretion and timbers in this area. When divers first encountered the wreck of *Beaver* in the 1960s and 1970s, they thought that the many bricks must have been dumped on the site. One theory suggested that the bricks were from the original Prospect Point Light, built on the site after *Beaver*'s wreck and later demolished in

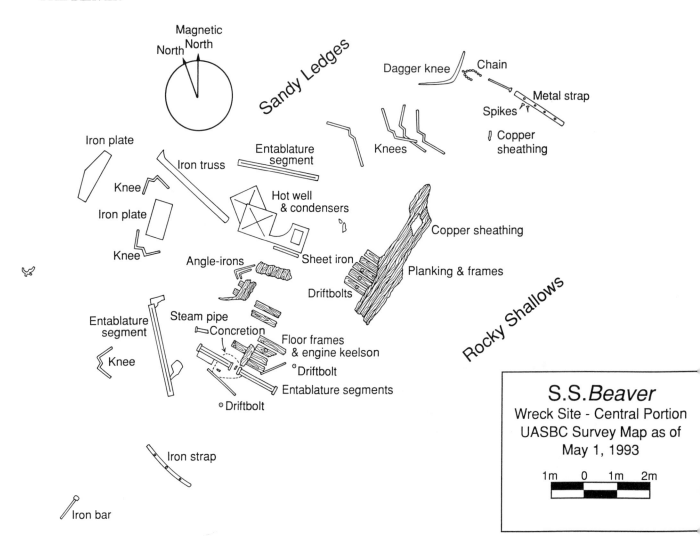

Map of the wreck. (Courtesy Underwater Archaeological Society of BC)

favour of a reinforced concrete structure. Another was that the bricks had been lost when a scow of construction materials capsized. Neither is true. Mapping of the bottom showed a relatively confined area of bricks, some still mortared together where they once formed the fireboxes for the boiler.

At least two, and possibly three, separate types of brick are located on the site. Red bricks stamped "Tamar," are firebricks of unknown origin. The others, yellow bricks stamped "T. Carr," are firebricks manufactured by the Newcastle on Tyne firm of Thomas Carr and Sons, which produced bricks of this type between 1827 and 1918. These firebricks, which lie scattered in a loose concentration around the engine remains, were broken loose when the hull disintegrated and were presumably scattered further by the 1908 recovery of the boiler, as their grouping is random and not in patterns that would indicate bricks tumbling along with the current.

How *Beaver* Broke Up

Despite the position of the wreck of *Beaver*, at a busy harbour entrance with strong tidal flow, it rested in a nonetheless protected marine environment, free of large waves and surges, for four years, allowing rust to form concretion, and giving marine organisms an opportunity to cement the hull into the rocks. It also fortuitously resulted in a wealth of photographic and artistic documentation of the wreck over that period; this provides a baseline of historical information from which to determine how *Beaver* was transformed from an intact ship into an archaeological site.

Photographs taken of the wreck from different angles, from 1888 until 1892, show slow deterioration at first. The ship grounded with its bow wedged in the rocks, its stern also in the rocks but in deeper water, and heeled to starboard. At high tide, the water came over the starboard bulwark and left the starboard paddlewheel submerged. Stripping of the hulk by souvenir hunters is evident in most photographs. A photograph of the engine room around 1890 shows the engines intact, the paddlewheel shafts resting on their plummer blocks, and the boiler in place, while the hull gapes open and large sections of ceiling planking and decking are missing.

The effects of deterioration and gravity are evident in photographs and drawings that date to 1891-1892. The boiler broke free of its mounts and tumbled to starboard, shifting the angle of the steamer's single stack.

Early 20th-century photographs of the wreck at low tide show the boiler rising above the surface. Based on the size of the boiler, it was resting at low tide in six to eight feet of water. The port paddlewheel shaft then tumbled, resting on the rocks with the mangled wheel in the water.

Despite the strong tides that sweep through the narrows, the majority of the ship remained at or close to the wreck site. The half-submerged decks and superstructure collapsed and were torn free on June 26, 1892, when the steamer *Yosemite* passed close by and threw up a large wake. The hull, weakened, broke apart.

The majority of the hull bottom is now buried beneath the pedestrian walkway and seawall, with portions exposed between the rocks. Despite the consistent efforts of determined salvors over an 80-year period, a large portion of *Beaver* survives.

CHAPTER SIX: THE STEAMER *BEAVER*

Beaver was laid down and built with a sailing-ship hull. Registered at 109 tons, *Beaver*'s engine room was rated at 78 tons (although it carried only 63½ tons of machinery) for a final tonnage of 187 tons. That figure included accommodations for 20 tons of coal stowed in "coal boxes," or iron partitions in the engine room, and a hundred gallons of fresh water. The boiler held additional water.

The hull was 101 feet long, with a 20-foot beam, although the 6½-foot-wide sidewheels increased the extreme breadth of the steamer to a more formidable 33 feet. The depth of the hold, from the keel to the deck, was 11 feet. The waterline was seven feet above the keel, but when fully laden, *Beaver* drew eight feet, four inches forward and eight feet, six inches aft.

Beaver was built primarily of English and African oak (which some later observers mistook for teak). The 11 x 14-inch, 100-foot-long keel, and the stem and sternposts were oak. The frames, which were 12 x 10½ inches in the engine room and nine by ten inches elsewhere at the floors, were all English oak, and spaced on two-foot centres. The massive hull was solid amidships, with the floors filled and reinforced by four 48-to 50-foot long, ten x 16-inch African oak sleepers, or engine keelsons, to support the weight of the machinery. The hull was reinforced with ¾-inch-thick, three-inch-wide diagonal iron strapping rabetted into the frames and held to them with copper bolts.

Beaver was built of wood described by the Lloyds' surveyor during the ship's first inspection in 1835 as "good quality, well squared and free from sap," with "good workmanship" throughout. The timbers were fastened with copper bolts and drifts below the waterline, and iron spikes above the waterline. The decks were supported by African oak and iron hanging knees. The outer hull was made of 2½-inch-thick elm planks to the wales, and then 2½-inch-thick

Contract for building Beaver.
(Courtesy Vancouver Maritime Museum)

oak planks up the deck. The hull was also sheathed with boards, tar, felt, and copper. [1]

Beaver was two-masted and carried a fore-and-aft rig; it was described in contemporary documents as a "schooner," but was actually a brigantine rig, with the foremast square-rigged. The foremast was 108 feet high from the keel, the mainmast 90 feet high. *Beaver* was fitted with two suits, or complete sets, of canvas sails, which were actively used throughout the steamer's fur-trade career on the coast. The rig was changed from a brigantine to a simple fore-and-aft schooner in 1838 in an effort to reduce weight.

The deck was flush, or open, with all accommodations below decks. The steamer was armed with five nine-pounder cannon for the coastal trade, which could turn hostile. One of these guns was removed in 1838 to lessen weight on deck when the ship's rig was changed. Boarding nets were strung along the bulwarks to keep away unwanted guests. *Beaver* was kept in immaculate condition. In one reminiscence, pioneer J.R. Anderson, writing in the Victoria *Colonist* on August 27, 1903, remarked that "having plenty of hands, the *Beaver* looked like a gentleman's yacht, every knob or gun polished, the deck likewise; in fact, everything, berths and cabins included, were as clean as elbow grease could make them, a creation of beauty and pride in our eyes."

Beaver's twin sidelever engines were each rated at 35 nominal horsepower and drove the two, 13-feet-in-diameter, 6½-foot-wide paddlewheels. The cylinders were 42 inches in diameter, with a three-foot stroke. Steam was produced by a low-pressure boiler situated aft of the engines and amidships, and placed atop brick fireboxes. The boiler operated at 2½ pounds per square inch. The machinery was described by Charles McCain, who salvaged a fair portion of it in the 1890s: "The piston-rod projected through the top of the cylinder to the centre of a sliding crosshead, at the ends of which linked rods ran down on either side of the cylinder to a pair of horizontal beams, or levers, which oscillated on a fixed gudgeon at the middle of their length. The opposite ends of these beams were joined by means of a crosstail, from which connecting rods led up to the crank shaft above. This shaft, six inches in diameter, was in three sections, and was thus supplied with four cranks, each of which was 18 inches in length." [2]

On the forecastle deck, the steamer carried a single log windlass of African oak, with iron pawl plates and pawls, as well as a capstan. The windlass handled the anchor cable, while the capstan was used for *Beaver*'s seven-inch-thick hawsers. *Beaver* was outfitted with three bower, one stream, and one kedge anchors, and 240 fathoms, or 1,440 feet of stud-link anchor chain. The anchors and cables were provided by the London firm of Hawks, Stanley and Co. of Pauls Wharf. The steamer carried two boats. Two plunger pumps on the deck, and a force pump connected to the machinery were on hand for emergencies; a hose connected to the force pump could reach throughout the ship and was available for firefighting.

Repairs and Modifications

During the steamer's five-decade-long career, *Beaver* was both repaired and modified on several occasions. The boiler was replaced five times.

The first boiler began to leak in 1839; it was patched for the steamer's 1840 trip to Sitka, but at year's end Captain McNeill wrote to his superiors to complain that "the boilers are getting the worse for the wear they are giving way fast and have patched in many places...." [3] Although pushed into service for another year, the boiler was clearly past repair. A new one was ordered from Boulton and Watt and shipped to Fort Nisqually on the chartered ship *Valleyfield*. John McLoughlin reported that the new boiler was installed by June 1842, but that 17 planks on the starboard side of the forecastle were rotten, and that work to ready the ship for a

Half hull model of Beaver *modified for passenger and naval service.* (COURTESY VANCOUVER MARITIME MUSEUM)

Half hull model of Beaver *as a towboat.* (Courtesy Vancouver Maritime Museum)

return to coastal duty would take several months.

The second boiler did not last much longer than the six-year life of the first. In November 1846, the H.B.C.'s officials on the coast wrote London that "the boilers are beginning to fail," and that a new boiler, ordered from Boulton and Watt and about to be shipped out to Fort Nisqually, would soon be needed. At the same time, "the hull of the *Beaver* is showing signs of decay." Captain McNeill had found "decay had commenced in many places, around the iron bolt heads. The forepart of the keelson also appeared to be injured," necessitating repairs. "It will no doubt be necessary," the report added, "to lay her up for a thorough overhaul and repair in a year or two hence, as she has now been running eleven years without any material refit...." [4] The refit did immediately take place, but *Beaver*, after ramming a rock at full speed off Point Chatham in Johnstone Strait, was beached at Fort Simpson. There, a 4½-foot section of the keel, 20 feet of false keel, the forefoot, and several sheets of copper were replaced.

A new boiler arrived at Victoria in June 1847 aboard the brigantine *Mary Dare*. It was stored there until August 1849, when *Beaver* arrived for a lay-up. The steamer remained at Victoria until mid-January 1850, while the third boiler was installed. It proceeded up the coast to Sitka in July 1850, where the Russian-American Company had a small shipyard, and there, over the next four months, they hauled *Beaver* out to replace planking and rotten wood in the decks and superstructure, and re-copper the hull. The log of *Beaver* notes that the Russians worked on *Beaver* again in 1851 and 1852.

The engines "being in want of various repairs," were overhauled between December 1853 and April 1854, when James Douglas reported to London that the engines "now go remarkably well, making 26 revolutions per minute, nearly equal to her speed when she arrived from England." [5] The boiler installed in 1849 was beginning to show signs of wear,

and at the same time Douglas forwarded the engineer's drawings for a new boiler to Boulton and Watt. The new boiler, *Beaver*'s fourth, was ordered in 1855. It arrived in 1856, and on March 3, 1857, Douglas wrote that it had just been installed. The engines were showing signs of age though, leaking steam from the cylinders and slides.

In late 1859 or early 1860 the engines were overhauled in Victoria, and at the same time the deck, formerly open for fur trading, was enclosed for nearly two-thirds of its length to the stern with a large superstructure. The new deckhouse provided staterooms and a large saloon for passengers. These cabins were modified in early 1863 by the Royal Navy at Esquimalt when *Beaver* was readied for hydrographic service.

The boiler installed in 1857 was wearing out by December 1864, when Lieutenant Pender suggested a new one would be needed within two years. A new set of square boilers was ordered in 1855 from the London firm of Low, Muir and Maudsley. They were shipped out and placed in the ship in July 1867.

Laid up in 1870, *Beaver* remained idle until 1874, when it was sold to private owners. For its work as a tugboat, *Beaver*'s last major modification involved the removal of aft portions of the superstructure to create a clear working space at the stern. At the same time, an elevated pilothouse was built atop the superstructure. In 1877, the steamer was hauled ashore and a new boiler, a Scotch Marine, and *Beaver*'s sixth, was installed by Victoria's Albion Iron Works. The steam valves were replaced with more modern poppet valves, which increased the engines' efficiency.

Beaver's upper works were damaged by fire in 1880; one account states that the superstructure was gutted. Photographs taken of the ship after 1880 show a different pilothouse than one in an 1877 photograph. The pilothouse was probably severely damaged or destroyed in the 1880 blaze, and replaced, but the nature and extent of other repairs are not known.

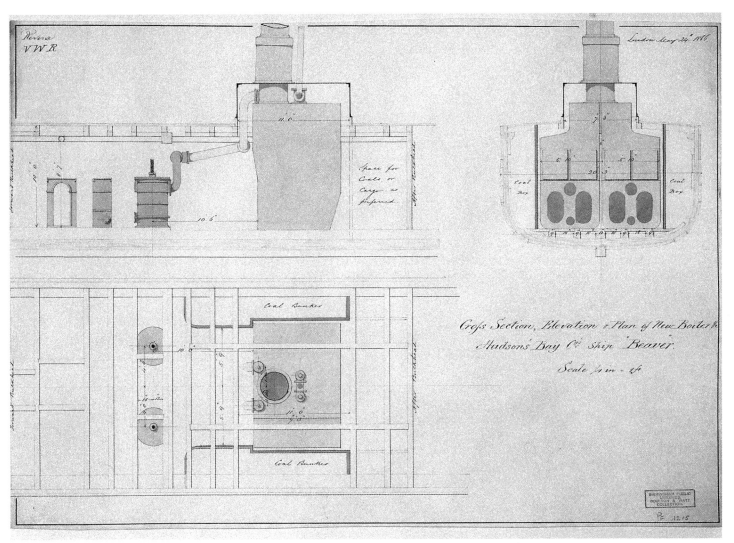

Cross-section of boiler. (COURTESY BIRMINGHAM PUBLIC LIBRARY)

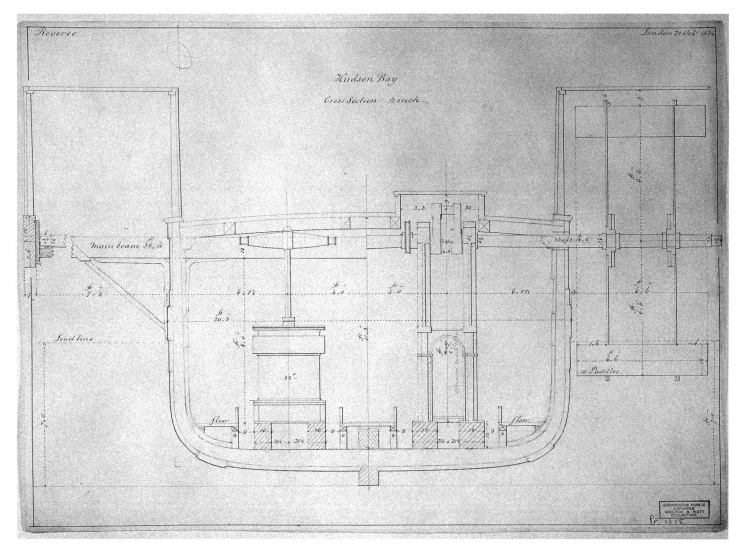

Cross-section of paddle gear. (COURTESY BIRMINGHAM PUBLIC LIBRARY)

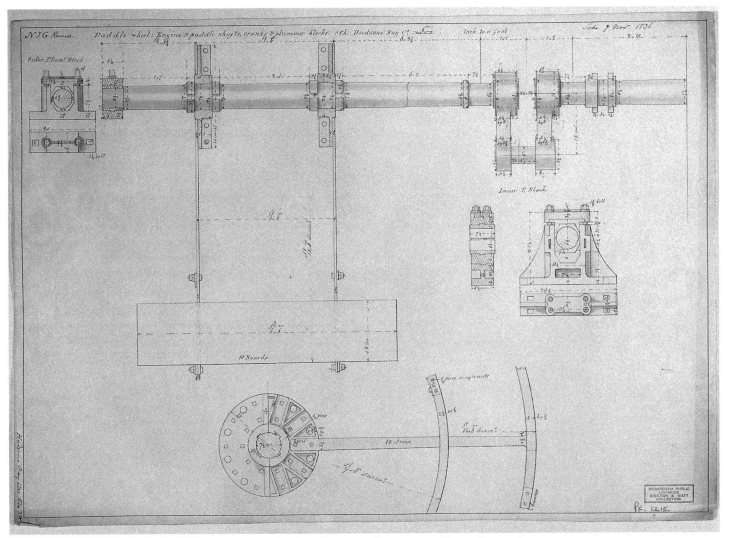

Details of paddle wheel. (COURTESY BIRMINGHAM PUBLIC LIBRARY)

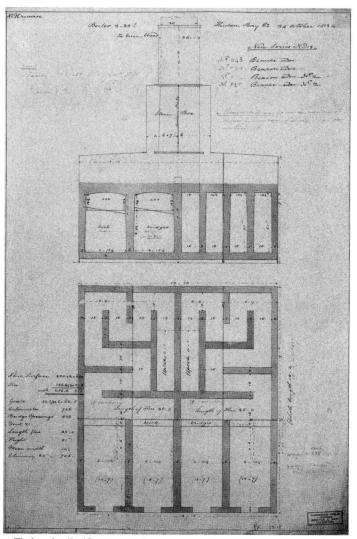

Firebox details. (Courtesy Birmingham Public Library)

When *Beaver* was wrecked in 1888, the boxy towboat bore little resemblance to the long, sleek steamer of 1835. Yet beneath the cumbersome superstructure, the oak hull and the massive iron engines remained strong and relatively unchanged. As *Beaver* broke apart and gradually washed away, they were the last to disappear.

Highlight: Characteristics of *Beaver*

Length: 100 feet, nine inches
Beam: 20 feet
Depth of Hold: 11 feet
Draft: eight feet, four inches forward, including 14 inches drop; eight feet, six inches aft
Tonnage: 187 tons (old measurement)

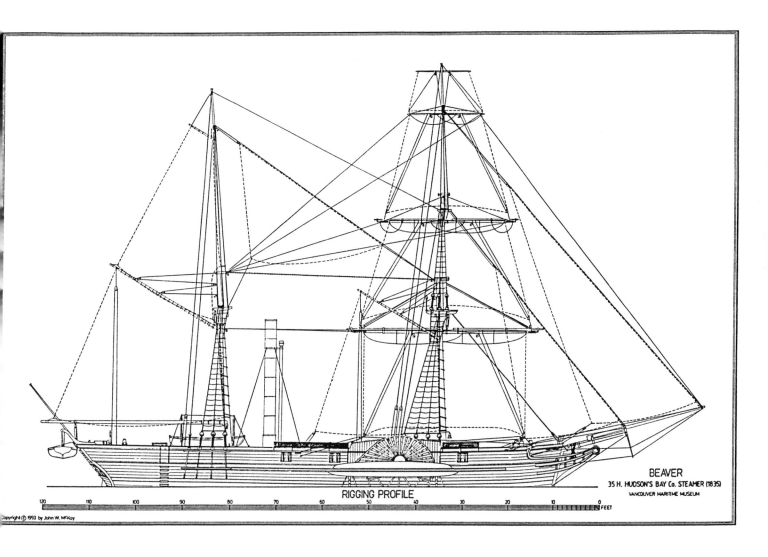

RIGGING PROFILE

BEAVER
35 H. HUDSON'S BAY Co. STEAMER (1835)
VANCOUVER MARITIME MUSEUM

120   110   100   90   80   70   60   50   40   30   20   10   0
FEET

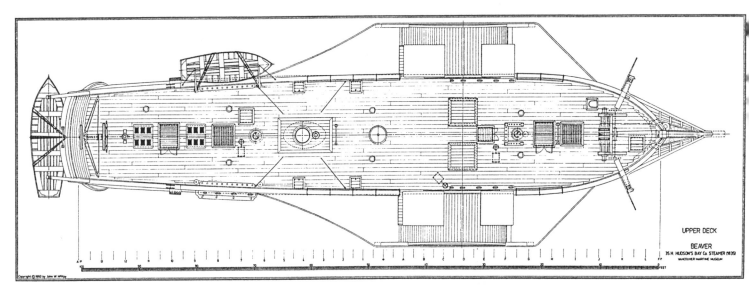

UPPER DECK

BEAVER
35 H. HUDSON'S BAY Co. STEAMER (1835)
VANCOUVER MARITIME MUSEUM

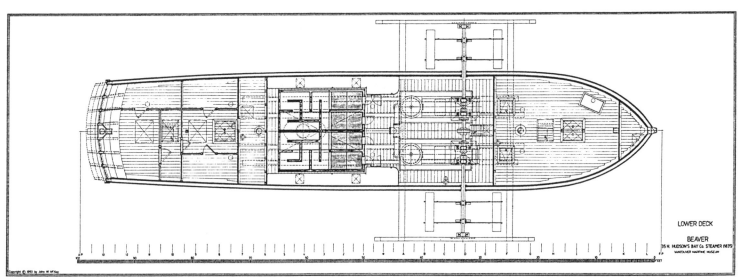

LOWER DECK

BEAVER
35 H. HUDSON'S BAY Co. STEAMER (1835)
VANCOUVER MARITIME MUSEUM

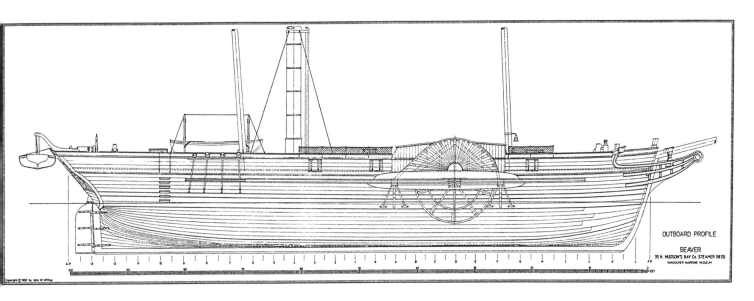

OUTBOARD PROFILE

BEAVER
35 H. HUDSON'S BAY Co. STEAMER (1835)
VANCOUVER MARITIME MUSEUM

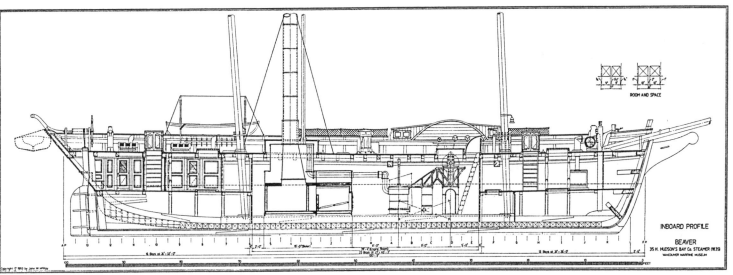

ROOM AND SPACE

INBOARD PROFILE

BEAVER
35 H. HUDSON'S BAY Co. STEAMER (1835)
VANCOUVER MARITIME MUSEUM

FOOTNOTES
Chapter One

1 Letter, Governor and Committee of the H.B.C. to George Simpson, London, June 2, 1824, H.B.C. Archives A.6/20, f.161.
2 Letter, George Simpson to the Governor and Committee of the H.B.C., Fort Vancouver, March 24, 1829, H.B.C. Archives D.4/93, f.71d-72.
3 Letter, George Simpson to the Governor and Committee of the H.B.C., Fort Vancouver, June 10, 1835, H.B.C. Archives D.4/102 f.28.
4 *Ibid.*
5 Letter, George Simpson to the Governor and Committee of the H.B.C., York Factory, August 10, 1832, H.B.C. Archives, D.4/99, f. 16d-17d.
6 *Ibid.*
7 *Ibid.*
8 Letter, John McLoughlin to the Governor and Committee of the H.B.C., Fort Vancouver, August 31, 1833, H.B.C. Archives, B.223/b/9, p. 21.
9 Letter, Governor and Committee of the H.B.C. to George Simpson, London, March 5, 1834, H.B.C. Archives, A.6/23, p. 123.

Chapter Two

1 "Contract for Building a New Steam Packet of 187 Tons for the Hudson's Bay Company," 1834, H.B.C. Archives, C.7/14, fo. 1.
2 Letter, William Smith, Secretary, H.B.C. to Messrs. Boulton, Watt & Co., London, September 20, 1834, H.B.C. Archives, A.5/10, p. 256.
3 Letter, Captain David Home to the H.B.C., Juan Fernandez Island, December 17, 1835, H.B.C. Archives, A.10/2.

4 *Beaver's* original logbook had disappeared, but was published, with transcription errors, in Lewis & Dryden's *Marine History of the Pacific Northwest.* I relied on W. Kaye Lamb's edited version in his article, "The Advent of the *Beaver,*" pp. 171-172.
5 *Ibid.*
6 Samuel Parker, *Journal of an Exploring Tour Beyond the Rocky Mountains,* p. 314.
7 George Simpson, *Narrative of the Journey* , p. 185.
8 Lamb, "Advent of the *Beaver,*" p. 174.
9 Letter, Duncan Finlayson to John McLoughlin, September 29, 1836.
10 John Fullerton, "My Days Aboard the *Beaver,*" p. 187.
11 John Dunn, *History of the Oregon Territory* , pp. 265-266.
12 Letter, Duncan Finlayson to John McLoughlin, Fort McLoughlin, September 29, 1836, H.B.C. Archives, B.223/b/12
13 Deposition of William H. McNeill, in miscellaneous papers, steamer *Beaver,* H.B.C. Archives, B.201/z/1.
14 *Ibid.*
15 Simpson, *op.cit.,* p. 188.
16 Dr. Helmcken's quotation has appeared in several publications, from an unknown original. I cite the version in Derek Pethick, *S.S. Beaver:,* p. 65.
17 Simpson, *op.cit.,* p. 236.

Chapter Three

1 Woodard's account is from McCain, *History of the S.S. Beaver,* pp. 48-49.
2 Letter, George Henry Richards to Dugald Mactavish, aboard H.M.S. *Hecate,* Esquimalt, December 16, 1862, H.B.C. Archives, miscellaneous papers, *Beaver,* B.201/z/1.
3 Dugald Mactavish to Thomas Fraser, Victoria, December 20, 1862, H.B.C. Archives, B.226/b/20, p. 329.

[4] Letter, W.F. Tolmie to Thomas Fraser, Victoria, January 25, 1865, H.B.C. Archives B.226/b/27 p. 188

[5] James A. Grahame to the H.B.C., Victoria, June 11, 1873, H.B.C. Archives, B.226/b/45.

[6] John Fullerton, "My Days Aboard the *Beaver*," p. 185.

[7] *Ibid.*, p. 186.

[8] *Ibid*, pp. 186-187.

[9] Donald H. Clark, "He Piloted the *Beaver*," p. 47.

[10] George Marchant, "The *Beaver*", p. 129.

[11] Letter, W.H. Evans to Major J.S. Matthews, as cited in Pethick, *S.S. Beaver*, p.104.

Chapter Four

[1] Elizabeth Winsby, "My Father Owned the *Beaver*," n.p.

[2] Charles W. McCain, *History of the S.S. Beaver*, p. 58.

[3] *Ibid.*, p. 68.

[4] Victoria *Colonist*, October 10, 1908.

[5] *Ibid.*

[6] Victoria *Colonist*, January 16, 1909.

[7] Vancouver *Daily Province*, January 9, 1925.

[8] Vancouver *Province*, February 21, 1951.

[9] Rogers' comments, later revised for publication in his book on shipwrecks of British Columbia, were first published in Pethick, *S.S. Beaver*, pp. 139-140.

[10] *Ibid.*, pp. 140-142.

[11] Vancouver *Province*, February 14, 1972.

There are no footnotes for Chapter Five.

Chapter Six

[1] *Beaver*'s characteristics are found in the "Contract for Building a New Steam Packet of 187 Tons for the Hudson's Bay Company," 1834, H.B.C. Archives, C.7/14, fo. 1.

[2] Charles W. McCain, *History of the S.S. Beaver*, p. 18.

[3] Letter, William H. McNeill to George Simpson, December 25, 1830, as reproduced in E.E. Rich, ed. *The Letters of John McLoughlin*, p. xiv

[4] Letter, Peter Skene Ogden, James Douglas and John Work to H.B.C., Fort Vancouver, November 2, 1846, H.B.C. Archives, B.223/b34.

[5] James Douglas to A. Barclay, Fort Victoria, April 26, 1854, H.B.C. Archives, B.226/b/11.

BIBLIOGRAPHY

Books

Dunn, John, *History of the Oregon Territory and British North-American Fur Trade.* (London: Edwards & Hughes, 1844)

Gibson, James R., *Otter Skins, Boston Ships, and China Goods: The Maritime Fur Trade of the Northwest Coast, 1785-1841.* (Montreal: McGill-Queen's University Press, 1992)

McCain, Charles, *History of the Hudson's Bay Company S.S. Beaver, A Pioneer of the Seas.* (Vancouver: n.p., 1894)

McCann, Leonard, *The Honourable Company's Beaver.* (Vancouver: Vancouver Maritime Museum, 1977)

Parker, Samuel, *Journal of an Exploring Tour Beyond the Rocky Mountains, Under the Direction of the American Board of Commissioners for Foreign Missions, in the Years 1835, '36, and '37. Second Edition.* (Ithaca, New York: Published by the Author, 1840)

Pethick, Derek, *S.S. Beaver: The Ship That Saved the West.* (Vancouver: Mitchell Press, 1970)

Rich, E.E., ed. *The Letters of John McLoughlin.* Second Series. (Toronto: The Champlain Society, 1943)

Sandoz, Mari, *The Beaver Men: Spearheads of Empire.* (Lincoln: University of Nebraska Press, 1964)

Simpson, George, *Narrative of the Journey Around the World in the Years 1841 and 1842....* (London: Henry Colburn, 1847)

Articles

Clark, Donald H., "He Piloted the *Beaver*," *The Beaver*, Volume CCLXXXIV, June 1953.

Farrington, Lawrence, "H.M.S. *Beaver*," *The Beaver*, Volume CCLXXXXI, Spring 1961.

Fullerton, John, "My Days Aboard the *Beaver*," *British Columbia Historical Quarterly*, Volume II, (3), July 1938.

Lamb, W. Kaye, "The Advent of the *Beaver*," *British Columbia Historical Quarterly*, Volume II (3), July 1938.

-------------, "S.S. *Beaver*: Vice-Regal Yacht of 1858," *The Beaver*, Volume CCLXXXIX, Winter 1959.

Marchant, George, "The *Beaver*: The First Steamer to Ply the Waters of the Pacific Coast," *Harbour and Shipping*, Volume I, (9) March 1919.

Winsby, Elizabeth, "My Father Owned the *Beaver*," *B.C. Magazine*, March 31, 1956, n.p.

Manuscripts

Beaver history files, Vancouver Maritime Museum, Vancouver.

Boulton and Watt Collection, PF 1215. Original drawings and correspondence, as well as the order books of the firm that supplied *Beaver*'s engines and four of the steamer's six boilers, in the Birmingham Public Library, Birmingham, England.

Hudson's Bay Company Archives, in the Provincial Archives of Manitoba, Winnipeg, contain the company's business records, including correspondence, several of *Beaver*'s logbooks, the contract for the steamer's construction, and miscellaneous papers including bills of lading, crew lists, registries and skin books.

Alaska-Yukon-Pacific Fair 29
Albion Iron Works 18, 42
J. R. Anderson 39
Annie 29
Aquaholics Diving Club 32
Peter Arthur 5
John Jacob Astor 1
Astoria 1
Edgar Crow Baker 22, 25
Henry Barrett 5
beaver 4
Beaver Cove 15
Beaver Creek 15
Beaver Harbour 15
Beaver Ledge 15
Beaver Passage 15
Beaver Island 15
Blunden Island 15
Bonwick Island 15
Boulton and Watt 5, 30, 39, 42
British Columbia Heritage Trust 30
British Columbia Towing and Transportation Company 18, 22
Edward Brown 25, 26
William Burns 5
Cadboro 2, 13
castoreum 4
C. H. Cates 26
Chitsekoff 6
Coghlan Rock 15
Edwin Coltman 18
Columbia 5, 6, 13
Columbia River 1, 6
Connis Islet 15
Convoy 7
James Cook 1
Cowlitz 13
Department of the Columbia 2
James Dick 5
Charles Dodd 16

John Donald 5
Cliff Donovan 31
James Douglas 10, 13, 42
Pete Dressler 32
John Dunn 7
Dryad 2
Empress of Japan 27
Esquimalt 15, 32
W. H. Evans 22
Duncan Finlayson 7
Fort George 1, 6
Fort Langley 3, 10, 13
Fort McLoughlin 6, 8, 10
Fort Simpson 6, 42
Fort Stikine 10
Fort Vancouver 2, 3, 6
Fort Victoria 10, 11
Fraser River 10, 13
John Fullerton 7, 18, 20
A. E. Goodman 25
George Gordon 5
Green, Wigrams & Green 5, 13
W. C. Hamilton 5
William Harrison 18
Hawks, Stanley and Co. 39
HMS *Hecate* 14
Dr. John Sebastian Helmcken 9
Henry Buck 20
George Holland 5
Captain David Home 5, 6, 16
Hudson's Bay Company 1-3, 5-7, 13-15, 42
Charles Humphries 16
International Brotherhood of Boilermakers,
    Local 359 29
Isabella 2
John F. Jagers 16
Julia Barclay 13
Labouchere 14, 15
Henry Labouchere 5

Mrs. John Labouchere 5
Alexander Lattie 6
Lou Lehman 32
Herbert G. Lewis 16, 17
Llama 7
Low, Muir and Maudsley 42
Uwe Maibauer 32
George Marchant 16, 22, 23, 31
Mary Dare 13, 42
Charles McCain 25, 26, 29, 39
James McIntyre 5
John McLoughlin 3, 10, 39
William Henry McNeill 7-10, 16, 39, 42
James N. Menzies 25
Charles Morton 18
Nisqually 7, 8, 10, 11
North West Company 1
Maurice O'Neill 32
Oregon Treaty of 1846 11
Otter 9, 13, 15
Pacific Fur Company 1
F. W. Pamphlet 31
Thomas Pamphlet 16, 18
Samuel Parker 6
Lieutenant Daniel Pender, RN 14, 16, 42
William Phillips 5
C. C. Pilkey 29, 30
HMS *Plumper* 14
Prospect Point 22, 24, 26, 34
Radius 30
Captain George Henry Richards, RN 14
R. P. Rithet 22
Fred Rogers 31, 32
Royal Canadian Navy 32
Royal Navy 14, 15, 42
Walter Rudek 32
George Rudlin 16, 18, 20
Russian-American Company 6, 10, 42
S. S/ *Beaver* Cruising Charters 32

Henry Saunders 18, 22, 25
Seaspan 30
Ed Seaton 31
George Simpson 2, 3, 6, 7, 9, 10
Sitka 10, 42
Gordon Squarebriggs 31
John Stafford 18
Charles Stuart 16
John Swanson 14, 16, 17
Taku River 10
Thomas Carr and Sons 37
Eugene Thurlow 20
W. F. Tolmie 15
Tongass 6
Underwater Archaeological Society of
    British Columbia 34
Valleyfield 39
Vancouver 2
Vancouver Maritime Museum 26, 29, 34
Vancouver Shipyards 30
J. D. Warren 16
Washington State Historical Society 29, 30
Whistler 18
J. W. Whitworth 22
William and Ann 2
John Williams 25
Frederick Williams 18
William Wilson 5
Charles Woodard 13
John Work 8, 9
YSP-126 32
Yosemite 37